Contents

T0385967

Welcome

1 Look and write the names of the characters.

Marta   Chris   Champ   Serena   Zero Zendell

1

_____

2

_____

3

_____

4

_____

5

_____

2 Look at Activity 1 and number.

a He is clever but a bit shy. He is Marta's friend. He likes school and does well in class. He is an excellent student because he likes studying. He hates getting dirty so he usually plays indoors.

b She is a very active girl who is not shy. She is brave and she lives in a nature reserve with her parents. Her parents work there so sometimes she helps. She's got a great friend. His name is Champ.

c He was in a tree and horrible wild dogs were trying to attack him. Marta's dad rescued him from the tree. Marta gave him his name and she looks after him. He loves Marta and they are best friends. He is happy and always friendly.

d He lives on Future Island. He always wears a top hat and he has got a long moustache. He is the only person who has animals on Future Island. He has a zoo. Many people came to the zoo but this year not many people are coming to the zoo. They don't want to always see the same animals. This is a problem for him.

e She lives on Future Island. She is a girl from the future. She is very active and is good at running and jumping, and she can climb walls. She is usually outside because she likes watching everything that people are doing on Future Island.

3 Look and tick (✔).

1 Who has a zoo?

 a  b  c

2 Who lives on Future Island?

 a  b  c

4 Read and answer. *True* or *False*?

1 Marta's dad rescues Champ from a tree. ____True____

2 Marta lives with her mum and dad in the nature reserve. _____

3 The name of the nature reserve is 'Elephant Rock'. _____

4 Marta is the chimpanzee's new dad. _____

5 The number of visitors to the zoo is going up. _____

6 Zero Zendell doesn't know what to do. _____

5 Complete the sentences with the words in the box.

> furry   sweet   loud   hard   ~~cold~~   spiky

1 The ice is _cold_____. 2 The chocolate is _____.

3 The music is _____. 4 The hair is _____.

5 The spider is _____. 6 The rock is _____.

6 (1:06) **Listen and tick (✓). Then write the object.**

> chocolate   a fish   a rose   a soft toy lion

	looks	feels	smells	sounds	tastes	What is it?
1	wet ☐ scary ☐	rough ☐ cold ☐	like the sea ☐ like a lemon ☐			_____
2		soft ☐ hard ☐		scary ☐ nice ☐		_____
3	brown ☐ black ☐	smooth ☐ sharp ☐	great ☐ bad ☐		sour ☐ sweet ☐	_____
4	beautiful ☐ bad ☐	furry ☐ spiky ☐	sweet ☐ good ☐			_____

7 **Read and circle.**

1 Chocolate (feels / tastes) (sour / sweet), (does it? / doesn't it?)

2 A fish (feels / sounds) (cold / light), (does it? / doesn't it?)

3 A rose doesn't (look / smell) (sweet / hairy), (does it? / doesn't it?)

4 A spider doesn't (feel / taste) (smooth / hairy), (does it? / doesn't it?)

5 A lion (smells / sounds) (soft / scary), (does it? / doesn't it?)

8 **Think and write.**

1   Shells are smooth.

2 _____ round.

3 _____ soft.

4 _____ scary.

5 _____ cute.

6 _____ loud.

Lesson 2 grammar (question tags)

9 Read and match.

1 Marta is brave,   **a** isn't he?

2 Chris isn't a bad student, **b** isn't she?

3 Serena isn't in the present, **c** is he?

4 Zero Zendell is planning something, **d** is she?

10 Read and complete.

> isn't he?   isn't she?   isn't she?   are they?   ~~is it?~~   isn't he?   isn't he?

1 Chris' hair isn't short, __is it__ ?

2 Champ is happy, _____?

3 Champ is scared of the dogs, _____?

4 They aren't excited about the zoo, _____?

5 Serena is a girl from the future, _____?

6 Serena is good at climbing walls, _____?

7 Zero Zendell is from Future Island, _____?

11 Read and practise. Write your own sentences.

1 The idea is terrible, isn't it?   2 _____, isn't he?

3 __He's very clever__ , isn't she?   4 _____, are they?

5 _____, aren't you?   6 _____, isn't he?

7 _____, aren't they?

12 Write about your partner. Then ask and check.

		My prediction	✓ or ✗
1	City/town	You are from ..., aren't you?	
2	Age		
3	Good at		
4	Pets		
5	Favourite Food		

13 **Read and sort. Where do these people work?**

> singer   secretary   gardener   hairdresser   receptionist   tour guide   chemist

Office/Building	Shop/Restaurant	Outdoors

14 **Read and complete.**

> policeman/woman   waiter   actor   ~~nurse~~   receptionist

1   She takes care of people in the hospital. She is a _____ nurse _____, isn't she?

2   He works at the reception. He's a _____, isn't he?

3   He isn't very shy, is he? He works at the theatre. He is an _____.

4   They are at the police station, aren't they? He is a _____ and she's
a _____.

5   He's very busy at the restaurant, isn't he? He is a very good _____.

15 **Write your own sentences. Use question tags.**

> tour guide   ~~gardener~~   secretary   singer   hairdresser

1   His garden looks beautiful. He's a ____ gardener ____, isn't he?

2   He is showing the city to some visitors. _____?

3   _____ in an office. _____?

4   _____?

5   _____?

16 **What do you want to become? Write about it.**

I want to become a _____ because _____

_____

_____ .

Lesson 3 vocabulary (professions)

17 Read and match.

1 tomorrow   **a** the week after this week

2 later   **b** thirty minutes

3 tonight   **c** today at night

4 half an hour   **d** the day after today

5 next week   **e** some time after now

18 Read and sort. Then write.

Monday   half an hour   later   tonight   tomorrow

See you … !	See you in … !	See you on … !

19 🔊 1:09 **Listen and complete.**

next week   later   tonight   half an hour   tomorrow

1 I'm leaving. See you _____!

2 The class starts at ten thirty. See you in _____!

3 Our next game is on Tuesday. See you_____!

4 I can't wait to be there. See you _____!

5 I'll see you in the afternoon. See you _____!

20 Read and write. What do you say …

1 to your family when you go to school? _____

2 to your friends when you go home? _____

3 to your teachers when classes finish? _____

4 to a friend that you're going to see next week? _____

1 Adventure camp

1 Read and complete.

Hannah   Tom   Felipe   Flo   Maria

 1

 2

 3

 4

 5

_____   _____   _____   _____   _____

Maria   twelve   love   British   football   can't   dancing   at   them   I'm   and   they

1 My name's Tom. I'm fourteen and I'm [1] _____. I [2] _____ playing basketball and [3] _____. I can cook and swim, but I [4] _____ surf. I have one sister, Flo. She's [5] _____ and she's very funny.

2 My name's [6] _____ and I'm thirteen. I'm from Mexico. I like [7] _____ but I'm not very good [8] _____ singing! I have two sisters. They're eight and ten and I love playing with [9] _____.

3 I'm Felipe. I'm from Spain. [10] _____ thirteen. I love playing video games [11] _____ I like Science and Maths. I have three brothers and [12] _____ love video games, too. We always have competitions.

2 Unscramble. Then label the pictures.

1 ttne   _____ (a)

2 surackkc   _____ (b)

3 geps   _____ (c)

4 rothc   _____ (d)

5 pomcssa   _____ (e)

6 isleengp gba _____ (f)

3 🔊 1:12 Look at Flo's list. Listen and write. (✔ or ✘.)

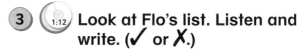

List for Adventure camp

a rucksack	☐	books	☐
a torch	☐	an mp3 player	☐
pegs	☐	a sleeping bag	☐
a compass	☐		

4 **Read and circle.**

1 I like (play / (playing)) football, but I (don't / doesn't) like camping.

2 He doesn't like (watch / watching) TV. He (like / likes) reading.

3 They're (Brazil / British). They're (live / from) the United Kingdom.

4 We're good (at dancing / dancing). We (never / always) practise.

5 She loves trampolining and (ski / skiing). She thinks they're (fun / boring).

6 He's good (at singing / at sing). He's a famous (soldier / musician).

5 (1:14) **Look and match. Then listen and check.**

a David Beckham   b Taylor Swift   c Lewis Hamilton   d Penelope Cruz

1 Who is good at playing football?   2 Who is good at acting and singing?

3 Who is from the USA and can play the guitar?   4 Who is British and loves fast cars?

6 **Write sentences with *good/not good* at using the information below.**

1 Sam / playing tennis ✗ _____.

2 Rachel / singing ✓ _____.

3 Andrea / dancing ✗ _____.

4 Peter / throwing a ball ✓ _____.

7 **Complete about yourself.**

My name's _____.

I'm from _____

in _____.

I love _____

but I don't like _____

I'm good at _____ and _____,

but I'm not good at _____.

8 Look and complete the sentences.

 ①    ②    ③

They're _pitching a tent_ .   We're _____   He's _____

_____ .   _____ .

 ④    ⑤   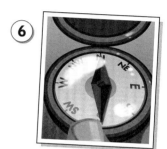 ⑥

We are _____   I'm _____   He's _____

_____ .   _____ .   _____ .

9 Look and write sentences.

1 The two boys _are pitching a tent_.   **2** The girl _____ .

3 The man _____ .   **4** The two girls _____ .

10 Look at the picture in Activity 9. Circle the things that you can see.

cars   compass   campsite   tent   pegs   dog   fire   sky   river

11 (1:20) **Listen and circle.**

1 I (can / can't) read a book, but I (can / can't) read a map.

2 They (can / can't) swim, but they (can / can't) pitch a tent.

3 They (can / can't) put in the pegs, (and / but) they can light a fire.

4 She likes reading comic books, (and / but) she (can / can't) read a compass.

5 We can pitch a tent, (and / but) we (can / can't) take down a tent.

12 (1:21) **Listen and write.**

Can	Can't
1 She can _____.	1 She can't _____.
2 _____ _____.	2 _____ _____.
3 _____ _____.	3 _____ _____.
4 _____ _____.	4 _____ _____.

13 Write.

What can you do?

_____
_____
_____
_____

What can't you do?

_____
_____
_____
_____

Lesson 4 grammar (describing ability; connectives *but/so*)

14 Tick (✓).

1 Where are Marta and Chris after traveling in the Time Machine?

☐ In the nature reserve.

☐ In a city in the future.

☐ In Zero Zendell's zoo.

2 Who has got Champ?

☐ Marta and Chris.

☐ Marta's dad.

☐ Zero Zendell.

15 Find and read Zero's code. Then write.

EHMYESGERCSSIT

TZIZ IZ MZ SZCZEZ MZSZAZE ZAZHZNZ.

_____

_____

_____ .

16 Read and complete the conversations.

1 Where are you going this weekend?

a We're going camping. Would you like to come?

b No, I don't.

c Yes, she's taking down the tent.

3 I can hear, but I can't see!

a Here's the map.

b Here are the pegs!

c Here's the torch!

2 Whose are these pegs?

a They are Felipe's.

b Oh, I can't read this compass.

c They are by the tent.

17 🔊 1:25 **Listen and colour the short vowels in red.**

1 chatted	stayed	planned	played
2 shopping	reading	hoping	hopping
3 stopped	booked	dropped	cooked
4 surfing	dropping	cutting	getting

18 **Read and complete the table.**

1 turn → turned, turning	**2** vote →	**3** shop →
4 work →	**5** stop →	**6** cry →
7 study →	**8** help →	**9** visit →

19 **Read and circle the short vowels in red and the long vowels in blue.**

1 Are you surfing or running this afternoon?

2 I stayed with Paul yesterday and we chatted about Mary.

3 He likes shopping and he doesn't like working!

20 **Complete the sentences with the correct form of the verb.**

1 My Mum and Dad _____ a holiday to Paris. (plan)

2 Yesterday we _____ football after school. (play)

3 In my English class we are _____ Harry Potter. (read)

4 Dad is _____ the grass in the garden. (cut)

21 **Read and complete.** after   rivers   seas   rainforest
deforestation   before

1 _____ areas as big as a football field disappear every minute. 2 _____

can cause drought which is a lack of water. This can cause the extinction of plant and animal

species in 3 _____ and 4 _____ . 5 _____ deforestation

there is no food or protection for animals that live in the rainforest. We must stop deforestation

6 _____ it destroys more of our beautiful planet.

22 **Read and match.**

1 deforestation

2 drought

3 rainforest

4 habitats

5 climate change

a lack of water

b dense jungle

c clearing of forests

d different weather conditions

e rivers, seas, rainforests, etc.

23 **Read and sort.**

drought   30 million species of plants and animals   hot and humid
dense jungle   the extinction of plant and animal species   climate change

Before deforestation

1 _____

_____

2 _____

_____

3 _____

_____

After deforestation

1 _____

_____

2 _____

_____

3 _____

_____

24 **Write. Find a solution to deforestation.**

1 What is necessary to solve the problem? _____.

2 What can *you* do to solve the problem? _____.

25 Read Pupil's Book page 19, Activity 21 again and match.

a

Luca

b

Alak

c

Melissa

1 Whose favourite place means 'the mountain with 300 peaks'?

2 Who likes camping in the summer?

3 Who likes visiting the largest National Park in the UK?

4 Who likes camping in the spring?

5 Who likes visiting a National Park where there are caves?

6 Who likes hiking to the top of the volcano?

26 Number the places (1–3) from your favourite to your least favourite. Then write.

☐ Vulcano ☐ The Lake District ☐ Khao Sam Roi Yot

My favourite place is _____ because

_____

_____

_____

_____ .

MINI-
PROJECT

Describe your ideal
camping trip.

27 Read and complete.

mother   help   good   but   reading
watching   run   kicks   doesn't   ~~brother~~

UNIT REVIEW

SEARCH

Two people I love are my mother and brother. My

1 __brother__ and I are good at basketball. We play every day.

My 2 _____ is good at football. She can't

3 _____ very fast, but she 4 _____ the ball. She

also loves 5 _____ romantic books and likes 6 _____ dramas on

TV. My brother 7 _____ like romantic films or books,

8 _____ he loves action films. He is not 9 _____ at Maths.

My mum and I can't 10 _____ because we are not good at Maths either!

28 Look at the email in Activity 27. Then complete the sentences.

1 My brother and I both like … _____.

2 My mum loves … _____.

3 My brother doesn't … _____.

4 None of us are good at … _____.

29 Write about your family.

My mum/dad/brother/sister … _____

_____

_____

_____

_____

30 Write about yourself and your partner. Use your notebook.

Me	My partner
What are you good at/not good at?	What is he/she good at/not good at?
What do you like doing/not like doing?	What does he/she like doing/not like doing?
Do you like camping?	Does he/she like camping?
What do you like doing when you travel?	What does he/she like doing when he/she travels?

31 Match.

1 tent
2 sleeping bag
3 pegs
4 torch
5 lay out
6 cover
7 compass
8 rucksack

a this tells you where north is
b put a bed on the floor
c use this to see in the dark
d this keeps you warm at night
e a house you can take with you
f you can carry clothes and books in this
g use these to stop a tent flying away
h put something over something

32 1:26 Read and complete the sentences. Then listen and check.

play   loves   running   sometimes   doesn't   ~~good at~~

I've got two brothers, Peter and Patrick. They're very different. Peter is ¹ <u>good at</u> swimming and he ² _____ surfing.
Patrick ³ _____ like water but he loves camping and ⁴ _____. He's good at skateboarding, too.
We often ⁵ _____ computer games at the weekend. It's the one thing we all love and ⁶ _____ I win!

I CAN
I can say what I'm good at and what I like/don't like doing. ☐
I can say what I'm doing now. ☐
I can use before and after to talk about the sequence of events. ☐

2 Wildlife park

1 Unscramble and match.

a
b
c
d

1 trote   _otter_
2 egrit   _____
3 sale   _____
4 tutelr   _____
5 eawlh   _____
6 hcthaee   _____
7 melur   _____
8 retpahn   _____
9 orinh   _____

e
f
g
h
i

2 Sort the animals from Activity 1 according to their habitats.

Jungle/Grassland	River	Sea
	otter	

3 🎧 1:29 Listen and write. Then match.

1 210
2 _____
3 _____
4 _____
5 _____
6 _____
7 _____
8 _____

a two thousand and ten
b three hundred and seventy
c six hundred and forty-two
d two hundred and ten
e two hundred and eighteen
f one hundred and eighty
g six hundred
h eight hundred

4 🔘 **1:31 Listen and write.**

		How tall?	How heavy?	How long?
1		1.2 metres	_____ kilogrammes	2.5 metres
2		_____ metres	60 kilogrammes	_____ metres
3			_____ kilogrammes	_____ metres
4		_____ metres	_____ kilogrammes	_____ metres
5		_____ metres	_____ kilogrammes	_____ metres

5 **Unscramble and write.**

1 hippo / is / long / how / the   _____?

2 tall / how / lion / is / the   _____?

3 the / heavy / snake / how / is   _____?

4 long / how / is / the / elephant   _____?

5 cheetah / how / tall / is / the   _____?

6 **Look at Activity 4 and write answers to the questions in Activity 5.**

1 <u>The hippo is 4 metres long.</u>

2 _____.

3 _____.

4 _____.

5 _____.

7 Complete the table.

1	big	_____	biggest		
2	tall	taller	_____		
3	heavy	_____	_____		
4	slow	_____	_____		
5	short	_____	_____		
6	small	_____	_____		
7	fast	_____	_____		
8	light	_____	_____		
9	long	_____	_____		

8 Look and write sentences.

1 The lemur is faster than the tiger _____.(fast)

2 The panther _____.(big)

3 The whale _____.(heavy)

4 The otter _____.(long)

5 The seal _____.(small)

6 The turtle _____.(slow)

9 Write your own questions. Then circle the answer.

> longer   faster   heavier   shorter

1 Are lemurs _____ than panthers? Yes, they are. / No, they aren't.

2 Are whales _____ than seals? Yes, they are. / No, they aren't.

3 Are whales _____ than turtles? Yes, they are. / No, they aren't.

4 Are camels _____ than gorillas? Yes, they are. / No, they aren't.

10 **Look and write.**

1 Which is the fastest? _____.

2 Which is the slowest? _____.

3 Which is the best swimmer? _____.

4 Which is the heaviest? _____.

5 Which is the tallest? _____.

11 **Write.**

1 giraffes / lemurs / rhinos (tall)

Giraffes are the tallest. Rhinos are taller than lemurs.

2 lions / whales / lemurs (big)

_____.

3 hippos / otters / seals (heavy)

_____.

4 cheetahs / tigers / camels (fast)

_____.

5 whales / rhinos / otters (short)

_____.

12 **Write sentences about the animals below.**

| rhino   cheetah   panther   lemur   camel   whale   seal   otter   turtle   tiger   giraffe |

1 Turtles are the smallest. _____.

2 _____.

3 _____.

4 _____.

Lesson 4 grammar (comparative and superlative adjectives)

13 Look and tick (✓).

1 Who can't Marta and Chris find?

 **a**  **b**  **c**

2 Who wants to help Marta and Chris?

 **a**  **b**  **c**

14 Read and complete.

on   Serena   friend   blonde

This is ¹_____. She has ²_____ hair and she lives ³_____ Future Island. She's Chris' and Marta's new ⁴_____.

15 Read and complete.

guards   thinks   price   chimpanzee   lost   time   friend

First, Marta and Chris meet Serena. Serena thinks that they are funny. She also ¹_____ that they are rich because they are looking for their ²_____.

Then, Serena tells them about Zero Zendell and his ³_____ machine. He wants animals at any ⁴_____ for his zoo. At the museum, they have to run away. The ⁵_____ are chasing them!

In the end, they are safe. But they are ⁶_____ and they can't find Champ. At least they have a new ⁷_____ on Future Island.

16 Read and complete the conversations.

1 Do you think you can help me with my homework?
  a I can't help it!   **b** No, it doesn't.   **c** Of course! Let's have a look at it.

2 I'm lost!
  a Do you?   **b** Don't worry! Here's a map.   **c** Thank you!

3 Be careful! You can't sit on the grass!
  a Oh! Sorry!   **b** Can't you?   **c** Yes, I did.

(17) **Read and circle the mistakes.**

1	SHORT	shorter	shortter	shortest
2	HEAVY	heavyer	heaviest	heavier
3	LATE	latest	later	lateest
4	BIG	biger	biggest	bigger
5	SLOW	slower	slowwer	slowest

(18) **Read and find two adjectives for each spelling rule in the box. Then write.**

> nice   big   new   heavy   happy   late   small   thin

1 -er and -est   _____ and _____.

2 -e + r and -e + st   _____ and _____.

3 Consonant + y   _____ and _____.

4 1 short vowel + 1 consonant _____ and _____.

(19) **Write eight sentences. Use the superlative or comparative of the adjectives in Activity 18.**

1 _____.

2 _____.

3 _____.

4 _____.

5 _____.

6 _____.

7 _____.

8 _____.

20 **Read and complete.**

| butterflies   dinosaurs   fur   insects   extinct   octopus   swan   wings   dinosaurs |

1 _____ lived a long time ago but they are all _____ now.

2 They can tell if the animal had _____ or not, if it could fly or not and many other details by studying the shape and the structure of the fossil.

3 The shape of the _____ of a flying dinosaur was not so different to that of a _____ or any other bird today.

4 There are fossils of big animals (_____, elephants, etc.) and fossils of very small animals such as _____ (_____, ants, etc).

5 Scientists can find out about the life history of the _____ by studying fossils.

21 **Read and match.**

1 A lot of information can be found by palaeontologists …

2 The life history of the octopus can be …

3 Marine fossils are also …

a … found under the sea by marine archaeologists.

b … explained by marine archaeologists.

c … when a fossil is found.

22 **Look and complete the table.** | octopus   wing   butterfly   dinosaur   leaf   insect |

1 Fossil of an	2 Fossil of a	3 Fossil of a
4 Fossil of a	5 Fossil of a	6 Fossil of an

23 Read Pupil's Book Page 29, Activity 22 again and match.

Helen

Laxmi

Carlos

1 The capital city is New Delhi.

2 The capital city is Buenos Aires.

3 The capital city is London.

4 Foxes have been seen in the outskirts.

5 There are wild monkeys in the parks.

6 There is a big nature reserve close to the city.

7 The national bird is the robin.

8 Cows and elephants are important in this culture.

9 Weasels can be found here.

24 Read and write.

SEARCH

Cool camouflage in the cold!

Size They are not very heavy and they are not very big. Their tails are usually about 30 centimetres long.

Body Arctic foxes have short legs and short ears. Their coats and tails are very thick and warm—good for living in the snow!

Colour Their coats are very good camouflage. They are white when it is snowy in the winter. In the summer, their coats are darker and change to brown or grey. It is difficult to see the foxes next to the brown rocks.

Places Arctic foxes live only in the Arctic, for example in Canada and Greenland. It is very cold there. They can live in temperatures of -50 degrees Celsius.

Food Arctic foxes eat birds, fish, and sometimes vegetables. They are good at catching birds—they are very fast! They often put food in the snow and then eat it later in the year.

1 Arctic foxes have white coats in _____.

2 Arctic foxes have brown coats in _____.

MINI-PROJECT

Write a fact sheet about an animal in your country.

25 Read and answer the questions.

SEARCH

PLEASE SPONSOR AMELIA!

Please sponsor me!

Amelia's story.

Here at the reserve, we have a lot of rescued animals. They live longer here and they are happier than in the wild.

Amelia the camel lives at the reserve. She's 175 centimetres tall. She weighs 80 kilogrammes. Amelia lived in the wild for years. Her home was next to a road and it was too dangerous for her.

We went on a trip to Morocco looking for ill camels. Amelia was next to the road. She was very ill.

Now, she is healthier and happier in our reserve. Please sponsor her!

1 Where was Amelia's home? _____.

2 Was Amelia happier in the wild? _____.

3 Was Amelia healthier in the wild? _____.

4 Where is Amelia now? _____.

26 Read, then write the questions.

1 Amelia lives in the reserve. <u>Where does Amelia live?</u>

2 Amelia's 175 centimetres tall. _____?

3 Amelia weighs 80 kilogrammes. _____?

4 She lives in the reserve because she was too ill to be in the wild.

_____?

27 Write.

1 Giraffes are _____ taller _____ (tall) than lions.

2 Rhinos are _____ (heavy) than cheetahs.

3 Cheetahs are _____ (short) than elephants.

4 Elephants are _____ (slow) than cheetahs.

5 Turtles are _____ (light) than whales.

28 **Read and answer.**

1 What is your favourite animal? _____.

2 What is interesting about it? _____.

3 What is its habitat? _____.

4 What does it eat? _____.

29 **Read and match.**

1 heavy

2 tall

3 fast

4 otter

5 seal

a opposite of slow

b an animal that can't walk but is good at swimming

c a good swimmer that lives in rivers and has a long tail

d opposite of light

e opposite of short

30 **Read and number.**

1

2

3

4

a Which is the heaviest land animal in the world? ☐

b Which is the tallest animal in the world? ☐

c Which is the fastest land animal in the world? ☐

d Which is the longest animal in the world? ☐

31 **Read and circle.**

1 How (heavy / heavier) is the elephant? It's 2,000 (kilogrammes / metres).

2 How (long / longer) is it? It's 2.5 metres (long / longer).

3 The panther is (bigger / biggest) than the otter.

4 Are giraffes (taller / tallest) than otters? (Yes, they are. / No, they aren't.)

 I can use measurements to describe the size of animals. ☐
I can compare and contrast animals. ☐
I can use and understand sentences in the simple passive. ☐

3 Where we live

1 Find, circle and write.

f	u	i	t	h	e	a	t	r	e	o	a	x	t
a	t	n	o	b	c	b	t	h	e	g	c	p	c
c	d	g	c	i	n	e	m	a	p	l	h	r	o
t	h	m	d	t	f	s	a	r	j	w	e	z	l
o	n	e	w	s	a	g	e	n	t	f	m	h	l
r	t	s	t	y	e	k	s	c	s	n	i	n	e
y	e	d	e	h	r	v	m	c	q	h	s	u	g
s	h	o	p	p	i	n	g	c	e	n	t	r	e

2 Read and match.

1 newsagent
2 cinema
3 post office
4 college
5 factory

a This is where you see a film.
b This is where you can buy newspapers.
c This is where products or goods are made.
d This is where you can post a letter.
e This is where you can study after secondary school.

3 Look and write.

1 I can buy shampoo in a _____.

2 I can find interesting animals in a _____.

3 I buy a magazine in a _____.

4 I can study in a _____.

5 I can watch a film in a _____.

6 I can buy some clothes in a _____.

4 (1:44) **Listen and write.**

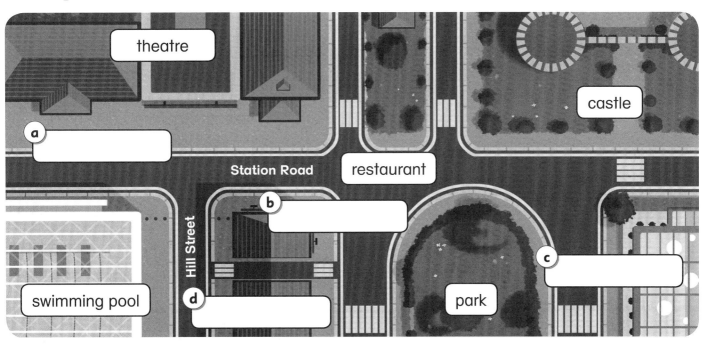

theatre

castle

a

Station Road

restaurant

Hill Street

b

c

swimming pool

d

park

5 **Look at the map in Activity 4 and write.**

1 cinema / swimming pool

The cinema is behind the swimming pool.

2 theatre / cinema

_____.

3 school / restaurant

_____.

4 park / shopping centre

_____.

5 castle / park

_____.

6 **Draw a map showing how you get from home to school. Then write.**

_____

_____

_____

_____

_____

_____.

7 Find, circle and write.

1

p	a	k	y	e	u	q	r	z	w	p	u	r	u
r	a	i	l	w	a	y	s	t	a	t	i	o	n
o	e	i	b	l	d	s	v	r	h	k	o	h	i
j	x	a	i	t	c	a	l	c	e	m	t	e	v
h	e	h	a	f	s	i	l	g	m	s	b	q	e
u	n	d	e	r	g	r	o	u	n	d	n	s	r
s	r	g	t	d	i	p	e	f	y	i	p	y	s
m	h	r	l	b	k	o	y	j	t	s	w	a	i
x	b	q	a	e	i	r	u	b	y	s	o	v	t
a	s	m	a	s	c	t	r	o	g	h	u	o	y

3

2

4

8 Read and match.

1 This is where you call when there's a fire.

2 This is where you call when there's an emergency.

3 This is where you can stay when you visit a new place.

4 This is where you can see your favourite sport.

5 This is where you wait for your bus.

a bus stop

b fire station

c stadium

d guest house

e police station

9 (1:47) Listen and complete.

> bookshop   bus stop   fire station   police station   university

Katy: Hello?

Michael: Hi, Katy! How are you? It's Michael here!

Katy: Oh! Hi, Michael! I'm fine, thank you! How are you?

Michael: Oh, fine, thanks. I'm just looking for the ¹_____ that you told me about. I'm in front of the ²_____ and I can't find it. Can you help me?

Katy: Of course! Can you see the ³_____?

Michael: Let me see…

Katy: There's a ⁴_____ and a police station. Can you see them?

Michael: Yes. Now I can see them.

Katy: Just walk straight ahead and you will find it on the right. It's very close to the ⁵_____.

Michael: Oh, I can see it now! Thank you very much!

Katy: You're welcome! See you tomorrow!

Michael: Bye!

10 Look and write.

1 Tom / go / park ✗

<u>Tom doesn't want to go to the park.</u>

2 Flo / post a letter / on Sunday ✓

_____.

3 Felipe / go / theatre / at the weekend ✓

_____.

4 Maria / go / circus / after school ✗

_____.

11 Look and write.

1 Tom / do his homework / on Sundays. ✗

<u>Tom doesn't have to do his homework on Sundays.</u>

2 Felipe / get a bus / everyday. ✓

_____.

3 Maria / go to the chemist / later. ✗

_____.

4 Flo / find / her theatre ticket. ✓

_____.

12 Read and complete.

1 If I g o to the shopping centre I will b u y new shoes.

2 If we go to Paris we will _ _ _ the Eiffel tower.

3 _ _ I go to bed late I _ _ _ _ _ _ tired tomorrow at school.

4 If it _ _ sunny tomorrow we will _ _ _ _ football in the playground.

5 If my sister passes _ _ _ test our parents _ _ _ _ be very happy.

6 If I don't do my _ _ _ _ _ _ _ _ _ my teacher will be angry.

7 _ _ _ _ only use the water we need _ _ will help our planet.

Lesson 4 grammar (first conditional)

13 **Look and tick (✔).**

1 Where is Champ?

 a  b  c

2 Who put Champ there?

 a  b  c

14 **Read and answer. *T*(True) or *F*(False)?**

1 Serena opens the door with a key. _F_

2 Serena has got a pet cat. ____

3 There aren't any real pets in the future. ____

4 Zero Zendell has got a zoo. ____

5 Chris and Marta don't want to rescue Champ. ____

15 **Look at the picture of Serena's house. Read and draw.**

Hi! This is where I live. It's in a noisy, busy city but I like it. My favourite thing in the house is the sofa. There's a TV opposite the sofa. I love sitting on the sofa and watching TV in the evening. There's a small table between the sofa and the TV. My dinner is on the table – it's fish and chips. I've got cupboards and a tall lamp in my room, too. The lamp is between the cupboards and the sofa. There's a picture behind the lamp, on the wall. It's a picture of some beautiful flowers. My bed is near the table and the sofa but it's not near the cupboards. But where's my robot dog? Oh, there he is! He's in front of my bed. He's hiding!

16 **Read and complete.** | hungry man dead real Champ animals

Marta and Chris go to Serena's house. They are ¹_____. Marta has a pet, but it isn't a ²_____ dog. It's a robot. Serena tells Marta and Chris that there are no animals on Future Island because they are all ³_____. The only person on Future Island who has ⁴_____ is Zero Zendell in his zoo. Marta and Chris realize that Zero Zendell is the ⁵_____ with the time machine. He's the one who has ⁶_____!

17 (1:53) **Listen and write. Use -ly or -ful.**

1 They found the cinema very (easy) _____.

2 Can you hear the music? The band is playing very (loud) _____.

3 The map was very (use) _____.

4 It was so (peace) _____ at the park.

18 **Write new words using the suffixes –ful or –ly.**

1 beauty __beautiful__   2 play _____

3 life _____   4 easy _____

5 careful _____   6 happy _____

19 **Read and circle the words with suffixes.**

1 Our guide was very friendly.   2 She played with the baby carefully.

3 'Can I help you?' she asked kindly. 4 You should talk politely to older people.

5 He ran quickly to catch the bus.   6 I visit my grandparents regularly.

20 **Look, sort and write.**

(friend)   (love)   (month)

(care)   (play)

Noun + *ful*	Noun + *ly*	Adjective + *ly*
	friendly	

(quick)   (day)

(strange)   (peace)

(careful)   (easy)

21 **Read and complete.**

1 If I __travel__ (travel) to London, I __will take__ (take) a map with me.

2 If you _____ (visit) a village, you _____ (see) a village church.

3 You _____ (get lost) in a city, if you _____ (turn) the wrong way.

4 If you _____ (be) in a village, you _____ (see) few people.

5 You _____ (have) more public services, if you _____ (live) in a town or city.

6 If you _____ (live) in a village, you _____ (enjoy) outdoor activities.

22 **Complete the sentences with 'used to'.**

1 Villages _____ (be) more populated in the past than they are now.

2 Cities and towns _____ (have) fewer inhabitants in the past than now.

3 In 1900 the rural population _____ (be) larger than the urban population.

23 **Look at the map and write sentences. Use words from the box.**

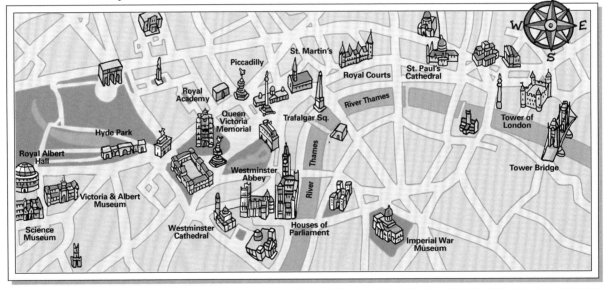

| bridge | corner | left | front | centre | way | right | north | south | east | west |

1 __The Science Museum is in the west of London__ .

2 _____ .

3 _____ .

4 _____ .

Lesson 7 maths (graphing population; first conditional, *used to*)

24 **Read and sort.**

Country, region or city	Homes	Interesting fact
Andalucía, Spain.		

1 ~~Andalucía, Spain.~~

2 Cave homes.

3 You can go sailing or fishing around the island.

4 Little white houses.

5 Tall buildings.

6 Hong Kong.

7 There are beautiful beaches and castles.

8 There are 7 million people who live in that city.

9 Paros, Greece.

MINI-
PROJECT
Write a flyer about your city or town.
What are some great things to see and do?
What is interesting about the place where you live?

25 (1:55) **Listen and write the places. Then write the answers.**

My town has a ¹_____ and a ²_____.
The ³_____ is next to the swimming pool. The ⁴_____ is opposite
the ⁵_____. The supermarket is next to the ⁶_____ and opposite
the swimming pool. The dvd shop is next to the cinema. It is between the cinema and the
hospital. The school is opposite the ⁷_____, between the ⁸_____
and the ⁹_____.

Today is a busy day. First, I have to go to the supermarket to get some food for the
weekend. I also have to go to the hospital. Then, I want to go to the ¹⁰_____
to get a DVD. If I have time, I also want to go to the ¹¹_____.

a Where does she have to go? _____.

b Where does she want to go? _____.

26 **Write sentences about where you live.**

My town/city ... _____
_____
_____
_____
_____
_____
_____
_____
_____

27 **Write about yourself. Where do you usually want to go or have to go?**

I usually want to go to _____.

I usually have to go to _____.

28 Read and write.

1 Where do you live? _____.

2 What is there to see where you live? _____.

3 Where can you learn something new where you live? _____.

4 What places do you usually go to where you live? _____.

29 (1:56) Listen and write.

near are small next to behind library restaurant want always turn

I live in a small town, but I like it. There aren't any shopping centres or cinemas, but there ¹_____ some restaurants and a lot of ²_____ shops. There is a good Chinese ³_____ ⁴_____ my house. There is a supermarket, too. It is ⁵_____ the swimming pool. I ⁶_____ to go to the swimming pool tomorrow with my friends. There is a ⁷_____, too. Sometimes I go there to get books. The library is near my school – go straight on from my house and ⁸_____ left. There is a small corner shop ⁹_____ my house, too. It's open late so I can ¹⁰_____ get things when I want them.

30 Read and circle.

1 If you want to buy books, you will find lots in a (*library* / *bookshop.*)

2 If you want to be on time, you will need to get a (*taxi* / *walk.*)

3 I will see you at the cinema if you want to watch a (*match* / *film.*)

4 If you want to post a parcel you will have to go to the (*post office* / *chemist.*)

31 Match.

1 a library   **a** you can fly from here

2 a supermarket   **b** you can get books here

3 a hospital   **c** this shop sells a lot of food

4 an airport   **d** nurses and doctors work here

I CAN
I can talk about what I can do and what I have to do. ☐
I can say where a place is and how to get there. ☐

4 Good and bad days

1 Look and write.

My favourite food is _____ .

2 Answer the questions using *every day / week*, *sometimes* or *never*.
Use your notebook

Quiz
1 How often do you have spaghetti?   2 How often do you have fish?
3 How often do you have fruit?   4 How often do you have biscuits?

3 Read and sort. Then circle the things you like and underline the things you dislike.

omelette   spaghetti   fish and chips   rice and beans   salad   biscuit   jam   sweets
sugar   soup   pizza   chicken   ice cream   cake   apples   banana   juice   cheese   fruit

Countable (How many?)	Uncountable (How much?)
apples	

4 **Write in the past.**

1 climb   <u>climbed</u>   2 cook   _____   3 drop   _____

4 want   _____   5 paddle   _____   6 fall   _____

7 sail   _____   8 eat   _____

5 **Complete.**

1

I _____ Mount Everest last year.

2

We _____ paella yesterday. It was difficult!

3

He _____ the plate on his foot. Ouch!

6 **Read and write. Then answer.**

> omelettes   was   loved   went   wanted   ate

Yesterday was a good day! A lot of people ¹_____ to the lake to do sports and I went with them. There was swimming, snorkelling, and kayaking. I ²_____ scared at first, but I ³_____ kayaking. It was exciting! I ⁴_____ to do it all day. I was with Tom and we paddled very quickly around the lake. There was a race with Flo and Maria and Tom was the winner.

After our day at the lake, we had ⁵_____ and salad for dinner. I ⁶_____ my dinner very quickly because I was really hungry!

Who is the writer?   Tom / Flo / Felipe

7 Circle. Then match.

1 miss (the bus / the bag)

2 eat (my juice / my lunch)

3 drop (the ball / the bus)

4 pass (a test / a curry)

5 pack (my test / my bag)

6 remember (my juice / my home)

8 Read and circle.

1 They were very hungry this morning so they (ate / didn't eat) some sandwiches.

2 Flo (missed / didn't miss) the bus yesterday. She was early.

3 Tom (dropped / didn't drop) the ball. He caught it.

4 Felipe (brought / didn't bring) his lunch. He had to buy a sandwich.

5 Last night, I (packed / didn't pack) my bag. I always pack it early.

6 I (passed / didn't pass) my Science test last week. I'm good at Science.

9 Read and complete in the past. Then match.

love   play   want   like   have

1 She _____ a lot of food on her tray. ☐

2 The woman _____ the film, but the boys _____ it. ☐

3 He _____ football last week. He was sad because
   he really _____ to play. ☐

10 (2:07) **Listen and number.**

a

b

c

d

11 Look at the pictures in Activity 10. What happened? How did it make them feel? Write.

a _____.

b _____.

c _____.

d _____.

12 Write about yourself.

| brought / didn't bring   passed / didn't pass   missed / didn't miss   dropped / caught |

1 _____. It made me _____.

2 _____. It made me _____.

3 _____. It made me _____.

4 _____. It made me _____.

13 Look and tick (✓).

1 Who didn't go inside the zoo?

 **a**  **b**  **c**

2 Who saw Champ?

 **a**  **b**  **c**

14 Read the sentences and write the questions.

1 Serena visited the museum last year. <u>When did Serena visit the museum?</u>

2 No, Serena didn't like the zoo. _____ ?

3 The assistant locked Champ's cage. _____ ?

4 Yes, Serena was in danger. _____ ?

15 Read about Future Island and complete.

> was   went   knew   year   climbed

Marta, Chris and Serena ¹_____ to the zoo. The zoo ²_____ very
big. Serena knew the place because she was there last ³_____. Serena
⁴_____ onto the roof to look for Champ. He was out of the cage. The alarm
went off and Serena left. At least, they ⁵_____ that Champ was alright.

16 Write. Use the correct tense.

> open   lock   drop   laugh   climb

1 He _____ his cage.

2 He _____ onto the table.

3 He _____ a chair on my head.

4 He _____ me in the cage.

5 He _____ at me.

17 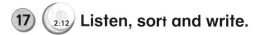 **2:12 Listen, sort and write.**

> played   visited   cooked   decided   washed
> followed   cleaned   landed   dropped   collected
> stopped   remembered   recorded   brushed
> studied   revised   listened   watched   sounded
> pitched   tasted   walked   covered   asked

/t/ sound	/id/ sound	/d/ sound

18 **Read and circle in red for /t/, blue for /d/ and green for /id/.**

1 I *packed* my bag in three minutes!

2 She *missed* the bus and *waited* for one hour.

3 He *dropped* the plate in the canteen yesterday.

4 His spaghetti *tasted* delicious.

5 We *cooked* together in the classroom.

6 They *borrowed* the recipe from their mother.

19 **Read and find the sound. Then continue the lists.**

1 /.../   watched, helped, missed...   _____, _____, _____.

2 /.../   covered, lived, learned...   _____, _____, _____.

3 /.../   visited, decided, tasted...   _____, _____, _____.

20 **Write sentences using verbs from Activity 17. Then read.**

/t/ _____

_____.

/d/ _____

_____.

/id/ _____

_____.

21 **Complete the questions and answers. Use words from the box.**

much　many　a few　a little　a lot of

1　How **many portions of** fruit and vegetables do we have to eat every day?

We have to eat **a lot of** portions of fruit and vegetables every day.

2　How _____ calcium have dairy products got?

Dairy products have got _____ calcium.

3　How _____ exercise is good for your bones and muscles?

_____ of exercise is good for your bones and muscles.

4　How _____ sweets and cakes should we eat?

We should only eat _____ sweets and cakes.

5　How _____ salt and sugar should we eat?

We should only eat _____ salt and sugar.

6　How _____ hamburgers and pizzas should we eat?

We shouldn't eat _____ hamburgers and pizzas.

22 **What was Emma doing right and what was Sam doing wrong? Write. Use verbs from the box.**

have a healthy lifestyle　do little sport　eat few fruits and vegetables
do a lot of exercise　eat a lot of fruit and vegetables　have a sedentary lifestyle

Emma	_____ _____ _____
Sam	_____ _____ _____

23 **Read and circle.**

1　Emma (was / wasn't) eating fruit and vegetables.

2　Sam (was / wasn't) doing much physical activity.

3　They (were / weren't) living different lifestyles.

4　He (was / wasn't) living a sedentary lifestyle.

24 Read the text on food traditions on Pupil's Book page 49, Activity 25 again and complete the table.

Country	Tradition

25 Compare your country with the UK. What things are similar? What things are different?

1 In the UK they have barbecues when the weather is nice.

2 In the UK _____.

3 In my country _____
_____.

4 Both in the UK and my country … _____

_____

_____

_____

_____

_____.

MINI-PROJECT

Make a poster about a special celebration in your country.
What do people eat?
What do people wear?

26 (2:13) **Listen and number. Then write.**

a She _____ yesterday.

b They _____ a big _____ last year.

c We _____ stew for _____ today.

27 **Change the verbs into the past.**

1 I cook stew. _____.

2 She paddles very fast. _____.

3 It makes me happy. _____.

4 He doesn't touch the ball. _____.

28 **Unscramble and write. Then match.**

1 didn't / he / the / bus / miss

_____

2 didn't / sunglasses / bring / my / I

_____

3 catch / she / the / ball / didn't

_____

3 sushi / make / didn't / we

_____

a because it wasn't sunny.

b because it was very fast.

c because we don't like fish.

d because he got up early.

29 Write.

My perfect menu	My partner's perfect menu
Starter: _____	Starter: _____
Main course: _____	Main course: _____
Dessert: _____	Dessert: _____
Drink: _____	Drink: _____

30 Read and match.

1 pack

2 spaghetti

3 drop

4 fish and chips

5 sushi

6 paella

7 curry

a a hot and spicy food from India

b opposite of catch

c fish and rice—popular in Japan

d rice and seafood—popular in Spain

e a type of pasta

f put things in a bag

g a popular food in the United Kingdom

31 Write. Use the correct tense.

drop talk play make walk cook miss eat

Last weekend was sunny. We ¹_____ football. We didn't win because our goalkeeper ²_____ the ball a lot and we ³_____ a lot of chances to score.

After the game, I ⁴_____ home with my friends to have dinner. My mum ⁵_____ stew, spaghetti, and chips. We ⁶_____ a lot of food! We ⁷_____ about the game and ⁸_____ our plan for the next game.

32 Write about what you did last weekend or last night. Use your notebook.

I CAN

I can talk about food from different countries. ☐

I can say what happened or didn't happen in the past. ☐

I can express events that happened over a period of time in the past. ☐

5 Arts and entertainment

1 Look and write the types of film.

1

_____

2

_____

3

_____

4

_____

5

_____

6

_____

2 2:17 Listen and circle.

1 Maria likes (romances / thrillers) because they are exciting.

2 She thinks she's too old for (cartoons / musicals) now.

3 Felipe loves (comedies / cartoons).

4 He doesn't like (musicals / comedies).

3 Write about yourself. Then compare with your partner.

I like these types of films.	I dislike these types of films.

Both my partner and I like _____ films.

Neither of us like _____ films.

4 Complete using the words in the box.

| didn't | had | saw | was | had | went | jumped |

Yesterday was fun. I ¹_____ to the cinema by myself.

I ²_____ a comedy. It was about a funny man, George. He

³_____ a lot of adventures with his dog. George always made

mistakes but the dog corrected them. It ⁴_____ really

funny. I ⁵_____ a good time. After the film, I saw Maria. I

⁶_____ out but she ⁷_____ see me!

5 Write.

| himself | themselves | herself | ourselves | yourself |

1 She went hiking by _____herself_____, didn't she?

2 You went to school by _____, didn't you?

3 He made breakfast for all the family by _____, didn't he?

4 She played a game by _____, didn't she?

5 They didn't buy the CD player by _____, did they?

6 We won the match by _____, didn't we?

6 Read and write the question tags.

1 Tom didn't see the film, _____did he_____?

2 Maria saw 'Shadow in the House', _____?

3 Flo and Maria didn't go to the cinema together, _____?

4 Felipe went with Tom, _____?

5 Maria and Felipe saw a sci-fi film, _____?

6 Flo liked the film, _____?

7 Read and sort. What family do these instruments belong to?

cello   harmonica   saxophone   triangle   drums   clarinet   harp   tambourine

Percussion	Wind	String

8 🔘 2:23 Listen and number. Then write.

a ⬜

b ⬜

c ⬜

d ⬜

e ⬜

_____   _____   _____   _____   _____

9 Write.

tambourine   jazz   band   saxophone   sing   sang   did

Bryn: Did you play the clarinet at the school music festival?

Michelle: Yes, I ¹_____.

Bryn: Did Jack and John play with you in the ²_____?

Michelle: Yes, they did. Jack played the ³_____ and John played the harmonica. We played ⁴_____ music.

Bryn: Did Alice ⁵_____? She's your singer, isn't she?

Michelle: Yes, that's right. She ⁶_____, and had a ⁷_____, too.

10 Write about yourself. Then compare with a partner.

jazz   rock   blues   pop   country   reggae   hip hop   classical music

I like these types of music.	I dislike these types of music.

We both like _____ music.   Neither of us like _____.

11 (2:25) **Make a prediction. Then listen and complete.**

	My answer	Cho
1 Have you ever written a letter in English?		Yes, she has.
2 Have you ever bought a CD by a foreign band?		
3 Have you ever made dinner for your family?		
4 Have you ever been late for school?		
5 Have you ever lost your keys?		
6 Have you ever missed a train or bus?		

12 **Read and complete.**

> yet   just   since   already   for

1 I've wanted that CD _____ a long time!

2 Have you seen my MP3 player? I haven't seen it _____ I left it on the table.

3 I've _____ remembered where I saw that film.

4 Have you finished? No, I haven't. Not _____.

5 I've _____ read that book. I read it last year at school.

13 **Read and answer.**

1 Have you ever been to a different country? _____.

2 How long have you been at this school? _____.

3 Have you forgotten to take something to school this week? _____.

4 Have you read an interesting book recently? _____.

Lesson 4 grammar (present perfect tense; ever/since/for/yet/already)

14 Look and tick (✓).

1 What can Marta, Chris, and Serena use to rescue Champ?

2 Who knows what is under the nature reserve?

15 Read and complete with a word from the box.

> zoo   closed   harbour   river   started   easy

1 Marta's parents _____ the nature reserve.

2 The nature reserve _____ 100 years ago.

3 There was an underground _____.

4 It was _____ to bring food for the animals.

5 The river went from the _____ to the nature reserve.

6 They used the river to get into Zero Zendell's _____.

16 Read and complete the conversation.

1 Where is the bookshop?

   a I'm not too sure. Let's ask.

   b It was closed.

   c They liked it.

2 You saw the film too, didn't you?

   a Did they?

   b Yes, I did. I liked it.

   c I would like to see it.

3 Have you finished the homework?

   a It was interesting.

   b I will go to school tomorrow.

   c Yes, I have. I finished it yesterday.

17 (2:30) **Listen and colour the prefixes.**

1	impossible	unhappy	invisible	untidy
2	dislike	recycle	disorder	preheat
3	invisible	unfit	prehistoric	incredible
4	retell	irregular	react	recycle
5	unhealthy	prepay	impersonal	precook
6	illegal	irregular	disappear	irresistible
7	immature	unusual	impossible	impolite

18 **Read. Then sort and write the words with the correct prefix.**

> ~~possible~~ happy visible ~~tidy~~ like cycle order heat formal fit historic
> credible tell regular act healthy pay personal cook legal agree
> appear resistible mature usual responsible write call polite

un-	dis-	im-	re-	pre-	i-	in-
untidy		impossible				

19 **Circle the correct prefix. Then write.**

1 (un- / dis- / pre-) healthy _____

2 (dis- / re- / un-) act _____

3 (re- / ir- / in-) regular _____

4 (re- / un- / im-) polite _____

5 (dis- / pre- / re-) cook _____

6 (im- / un- / in-) formal _____

20 **Read. Then complete.**

> unfair rewrite disagree preheat irresponsible

1 This rule is very _____.

2 I _____ with you!

3 It's _____ not to recycle.

4 I have to _____ my presentation on wild animals.

5 To cook this pizza you have to _____ the oven.

21 Read and match.

1 Pop music …	a …has a very complicated rhythm.
2 Rock …	b …is influenced by African music.
3 Classical music …	c …was very popular in 1970s in the USA.
4 Disco …	d …is also called popular music.
5 Jazz …	e …is often played at concerts by large orchestras.
6 Blues music …	f …is a type of music that you can dance to.
7 Country music …	g …is played with the guitar, drum and bass.

22 Read and complete.

1 I was _____ (listen) to a country song when she _____ (start) singing.

2 They were _____ (go) to a pop concert the day I _____ (meet) them.

3 My father was _____ (listen) to a blues tape when the lights _____ (go) out.

4 She was _____ (play) a jazz solo on the guitar when the people _____ (start) to clap.

5 The rock band was _____ (perform) my favourite song when my mobile phone _____ (ring).

23 Read the text again on Pupil's Book page 58. Answer *True* or *False*.

1 Jazz music has an easy rhythm to follow. _____

2 Blues was born in the United Kingdom. _____

3 Country singers usually write their own songs. _____

4 There is only one type of rock music. _____

5 Pop music is popular with young people. _____

6 Blues was influenced by music from Africa. _____

7 Folk and gospel are the roots of country music. _____

8 Pop music isn't commercial music. _____

24 Read Pupil's Book page 59 Activity 24 again and complete the table.

Name of the instrument	Country	Made of	When do people play it?

25 What are they made of? Look and write.

> is / are made of
> glass   metal   paper   plastic   wood   wool

1 This bottle   is made of glass.

2 This bag is   _____ .

3 This jumper   _____ .

4 This chair   _____ .

5 This book   _____ .

6 These boxes   _____ .

MINI-
PROJECT

Write a report about instruments around the world.

26   Listen and tick (✓). Then complete.

	make a cake	write birthday cards	say 'Happy Birthday!'	go to the theatre	see dancers
Flo					
Tom					
Mum					

My birthday last year ¹_____ great. My mum ²_____ a cake for me.

Tom ³_____ a nice birthday card and everyone ⁴_____ 'Happy

birthday!' I ⁵_____ very happy. Mum ⁶_____ tickets for 'Cats' and

Mum and I ⁷_____ the next day. We ⁸_____ the dancers and

⁹_____ some great music. I ¹⁰_____ it!

27 Read and ask questions.

1 I've forgotten something. <u>What have you forgotten?</u>_____.

2 My aunt has sent me an email. _____.

3 Everyone has just heard about it. _____.

4 I haven't met him yet. _____.

28 Write about yourself.

1 I've cooked _____.

2 I've never _____.

3 I've dreamed about _____.

4 I've been to _____.

29 Read and write the question tags. For number 4, write your own question.

1 She studied very hard, _____?

2 It didn't rain last week, _____?

3 You didn't comb your hair, _____?

4 _____?

30 Read and answer.

1 Have you ever played an instrument?

_____.

2 Have you ever seen a thriller?

_____.

3 Have you seen a good film recently?

_____.

31 Match.

1 cello   a You blow into this small instrument.

2 harmonica   b A type of music that started in the south of the United States.

3 saxophone   c A band usually has some of these. You have to hit them.

4 triangle   d You can play this using one hand, shaking it or hitting it.

5 blues   e A metal instrument that you blow.

6 clarinet   f A large string instrument that you play using your fingers and a bow.

7 drums

8 tambourine   g A metal instrument that has three sides.

     h You blow into this wooden instrument.

32 Read and complete. Then write your own pair of sentences.

themselves   myself   ourselves

1 She read the book on her own.   She read the book by herself.

2 We played the instruments on our own.   _____.

3 They liked the thriller that they watched on their own.   _____.

4 I can turn on the T.V on my own.   _____.

5 _____   _____.

6 _____   _____.

I CAN

I can talk about who did something. ☐

I can talk about what I have done. ☐

I can understand and use question tags in the past. ☐

6 Trips

1 Write.

 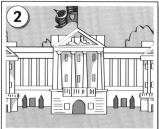  

_____   _____   _____   _____

_____   _____   _____

2 Write. Use words from Activity 1.

1 We went to the _____. There were a lot of fish there.

2 The _____ was great. We camped on Friday and Saturday night.

3 We loved the _____ because we love swimming.

4 The _____ was great! We climbed over the old walls.

5 The _____ was fun. I was sometimes scared, but it was exciting!

6 The _____ was fun, but the queen wasn't there.

7 I liked the _____. There were lots of dinosaurs there!

3 Write about yourself. Use words from Activity 1.

I love going to the _____ and _____.

I like _____,

but I don't _____.

4 Match.

1 What will you do at the library?

2 What will you do at the bank?

3 What will you do at the sports stadium?

4 What will you do at the museum?

5 What will you do at the aquarium?

6 What will you do at the National Park?

a I'll get some money.

b First, I'll get some books for school. Then, I'll go on the Internet.

c First, I'll go to the dinosaur room. Then, I'll go to the insect room.

d I'll see lots of beautiful fish.

e First, I'll pitch the tent. Then, I'll go kayaking.

f I'll watch a football match.

5 Write.   snorkelling   rollerblading   horse riding   skateboarding   rock climbing   surfing

1 First, I'll go _snorkelling_____.

Then, I'll go _____.

2 First, _____.

Then, _____.

3 _____.

_____.

6 Unscramble and answer.

1 what / will / after / do / you / school? _____?

_____.

2 go / weekend / where / will / you / at / the? _____?

_____.

3 your / on / trip / will / go / where / you? _____?

_____.

7 Write about a partner. Use the questions from Activity 6.

_____

_____.

8 Write. Then find.

1

_____

2

_____

3

_____

a	r	o	l	l	e	r	c	o	a	s	t	e	r
p	t	i	n	i	a	m	i	n	i	g	o	l	f
i	z	b	b	e	r	c	f	p	q	j	d	i	g
r	b	l	o	r	b	i	g	w	h	e	e	l	k
a	f	s	a	r	e	m	v	a	w	y	z	t	k
t	f	n	t	g	o	s	d	t	c	l	u	s	c
e	d	k	i	q	a	h	i	e	e	d	h	n	l
s	o	i	n	g	b	c	a	r	o	u	s	e	l
h	d	l	g	f	n	x	d	s	o	b	e	v	t
i	g	m	l	n	f	w	m	l	f	b	n	k	j
p	e	w	a	t	b	k	u	i	r	g	u	p	x
x	m	o	k	y	j	c	u	d	l	v	m	w	t
p	s	z	e	a	b	b	l	e	b	w	a	t	s

4

_____

5

_____

6

_____

9 There are two more places in Activity 8. Find them and write.

My favourite ride is the _____.

I also like playing _____ with my friends.

10 Read and complete. Then match.

| like   dance   watch   play   go |

1 Will they _____ the chocolate cake?

2 Will they _____ football tomorrow?

3 Will they _____ to the aquarium?

4 Will they _____ a funny film?

5 Will they _____ at the school disco?

a I'm not sure. The weather won't be sunny.

b No, they won't. They like scary films.

c Yes, they will. They love watching the fish.

d Yes, they will. They really love music.

e I'm sure they will. They love sweet things.

Lesson 3 vocabulary (amusement park attractions)

11 (2:40) **Listen and complete.**

| shall   water park   much   else   could   where |

Louise: Hi, Pamela! ¹_____ we go out?

Pamela: OK, ²_____ can we go?

Louise: Shall we go to the ³_____?

Pamela: I don't like swimming very ⁴_____. Where ⁵_____ could we go?

Louise: If you like animals, we ⁶_____ go to the Natural History Museum.

Pamela: Great! I haven't been there yet!

12 **Read and match.**

1 What time shall we meet?

2 Where shall we have lunch?

3 Shall I open the window?

4 Shall we go to the cinema tonight

5 I've left my lunch at home

a Yes, please. It is too warm!

b What about 10 o'clock?

c I'm sorry but I'm having dinner with my grandparents.

d You should buy a sandwich from the canteen.

e There's a new restaurant by the university. Shall we try it?

13 **Write your own sentences.**

1 Shall we _____?

2 What else _____?

3 We could _____.

4 She could _____.

5 I'm hungry! Shall we _____?

6 It's raining. We could _____.

7 They could _____.

8 Could he _____?

Lesson 4 grammar (suggestions: *shall/could*)

STORY

14 **Look and tick (✓).**

1 Who is not telling the truth?

 a  b  c

2 Where did Zero say he found the chimpanzee?

 a  b  c

15 (2:42) **Listen and write.**

1

Last year, I _____ the sea to South America.

2

I _____ a mountain.

3

I _____ into the rainforest.

4

I _____ a very tall tree.

5

I _____ a special cage.

6

And I _____ the last dodo in the world!

16 **Make three predictions about Future Island.**

1 I think that Marta and Chris will _____.

2 I think that Zero Zendell will _____.

3 I think that Champ will _____.

17 **Read the sentences and complete the conversation.**

1 Shall we go to the zoo? | a Yes, I did | b Sure! Let's go! | c Yes, he will

2 There aren't any tickets left. | a That's a pity! | b Aren't they? | c Yes, it is.

3 Will you go on a trip this summer? | a No, it won't. | b Yes, I do. | c Yes, I will.

18 (2:46) **Listen. Then draw the arrow up or down.**

↗ rising intonation   ↘ falling intonation

1 She isn't having dinner with us, is she? ☐

2 John came to the party, didn't he? ☐

3 It's cold today, isn't it? ☐

4 You are visiting your grandad, aren't you? ☐

5 They didn't enjoy the party, did they? ☐

6 It isn't a very good film, is it? ☐

19 **Read and complete.**

1 You are coming with us, _aren't you?_ .

2 This book is very boring, _____?

3 You revised a lot for the test, _____?

4 She doesn't play the piano, _____?

5 It is a very hot day, _____?

6 You like the new teacher, _____?

7 They won't go on holiday this summer, _____?

8 He would like a cup of coffee, _____?

20 (2:47) **Listen and complete. Then draw an arrow up or down.**

1 Your sister enjoyed the party, _____? ☐

2 They can come together, _____? ☐

3 You are joking, _____? ☐

4 It was very hot yesterday, _____? ☐

5 Peter wants to come with us, _____? ☐

21 **Write three sentences. Use question tags. Then read.**

1 _____?

2 _____?

3 _____?

22 Read and complete.

storms   drought   snows   rain   fog

The weather can be wet or dry. In summer, there can be a ¹_____ if it doesn't
rain for a long time. In winter, the weather is wet with lots of ²_____, especially
in the UK. If there is ³_____, you may not be able to see what's in front of you!
When it's very cold it often ⁴_____, and so you can play and make snowmen.
In tropical countries they often have big ⁵_____.

23 Sort these activities.

skiing   watching a film   diving   reading a book   swimming   making a snowman

Snowy weather	Sunny weather	Rainy weather

24 Unscramble the sentences. Then match.

1 sky / very / the / is / cloudy / today

_____.

a snowman / we / make / can / a

_____.

2 temperature / high / very / the / is

_____.

b use / we / less / may / have to / water

_____.

3 window / please / hot / it's / I / may / the
/ open

_____?

c football / play / I / might

_____.

4 snows / it / if / lot / a

_____.

d course / of

_____.

5 my / finish / if / homework / I

_____.

e snow / not / it / might

_____.

6 there / a / drought / if / is

_____.

f rain / tomorrow / it / may

_____.

25 **Read Pupil's Book page 69 again and complete the table. Then write two more details for each place.**

1 There are beautiful fairy chimneys here.

2 It is a lost city in the Andean mountains.

3 You can find the tomb of an emperor and a princess here.

Machu Picchu	Taj Mahal	Cappadocia
•	•	•
•	•	•
•	•	•

26 **What do you do when you travel? Write ✓ or ✗.**

1 I write emails to my family. ☐

2 I send letters to my family. ☐

3 I read guidebooks. ☐

4 I keep a diary of my journey. ☐

5 I get nervous when I am on a flight. ☐

6 I buy presents for my friends. ☐

7 I take lots of photographs. ☐

MINI-
PROJECT

Think of a nice place to visit where you live. Make a poster to describe it.

27 **Read and circle.**

1 Shall we (*went* / *go* / *will*) to the cinema?

2 What else could we (*seen* / *saw* / *see*) at the museum?

3 They could go (*on* / *in* / *under*) the big wheel.

4 Shall we visit the castle (*in* / *on* / *under*) Tuesday?

28 **Look and write.**

1 _____

2 _____

3 _____

4 _____

5 _____

6 _____

7 _____

8 _____

9 _____

10 _____

tourist	letter	diary	journey	passenger
envelope	guidebook	taxi	stamp	flight

29 **Write sentences. Use words from Activity 28.**

1 I will write you a letter from England _____ .

2 _____ .

3 _____ .

4 _____ .

5 _____ .

6 _____ .

7 _____ .

29 **Write sentences about yourself.**

1 What do you think you will do next summer?

_____.

2 How will you get there?

_____.

3 What will you do first?

_____.

4 What will you do next?

_____.

5 Why do you want to go there?

_____.

30 **Match.**

1 dodgems

2 an aquarium

3 boating lake

4 amusement park

5 rollercoaster

6 stadium

7 National Park

8 water slide

9 museum

a You can go on a boat here.

b This is a big natural area in the mountains or forest.

c Children can drive these.

d You can study History and Art here.

e This is fast and wet!

f This takes you high up in the sky!

g You can see lots of types of fish here.

h Teams play sports here.

i This is a fun place. There are many rides here.

31 **Write.**

1 What did you do yesterday?

_____.

2 What will you do tomorrow?

First, _____.

Then, _____.

I CAN I can make predictions and talk about unplanned events. ☐

I can make suggestions. ☐

7 Space

1 Match. Then write.

1 tele 2 astro 3 space 4 space   a en   b et   c station   d met

5 pla   e sters

6 rock 7 ali 8 co 9 boo   i ship   h scope   g naut   f net

1 <u>telescope</u>   4 _____   7 _____
2 _____   5 _____   8 _____
3 _____   6 _____   9 _____

2 🔊 3:03 Look and listen. Then match.

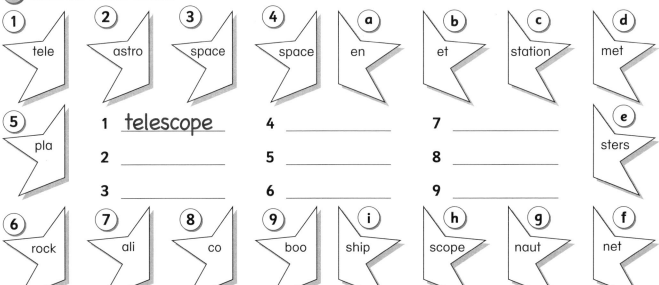

1 What is the fourth planet from the Sun?   a Mars
2 What is the third planet from the Sun?   b Earth
3 What is the fifth planet from the Sun?   c Jupiter
4 What is the eighth planet from the Sun?   d Neptune
5 What is the second planet from the Sun?   e Venus

3 Write.

1 The astronaut is in the _____.

2 The astronaut is angry because there are _____ in the spaceship.

3 He doesn't know _____ they got into the spaceship.

4 Alien A has a _____.

5 Alien B is _____ on the astronaut's spacesuit!

4 Read and complete.

should / need to

1 You _____ go to school every day.

2 They _____ learn about the solar system. It's very interesting.

3 She _____ see the new Star Wars film. She will like it.

4 You _____ call an ambulance. She doesn't feel well.

5 Plants _____ have water to live.

6 He _____ do his homework before he watches TV.

5 Unscramble and write.

1 ought / try / you / to / astronaut's / food

_____.

2 better / you'd / turn / off / television / the

_____.

3 he / astronomy / study / should

_____.

4 doesn't / he / to / need / take / telescope / his

_____.

6 Read. Then write the questions.

1 I need to do my homework every day.

   How often do you need to do your homework?

2 They should try the new restaurant because it's amazing.

_____?

3 We'd better hurry up because we might be late.

_____?

4 It's our teacher who says we need to take more tests.

_____?

7 **Look at the table. Then write. Where do these words go?**

| important | exciting | scary | frightening | tall | kind |
| intelligent | difficult | pretty | complicated | small | clever |

one or two syllables [big / ea-sy]	three syllables or more [a-ma-zing]

8 **Read and write ✓ if you agree or ✗ if you disagree.**

1   Sci-fi films are more exciting than cartoons. ☐

2   Football is more complicated than basketball. ☐

3   Amusement parks are more amazing than National Parks. ☐

4   Elephants are more frightening than tigers. ☐

5   Maths is more important than English. ☐

9 **Make up four sentences of your own. Use the word bank.**

| important | interesting | expensive | horrible |

1   _____ .

2   _____ .

3   _____ .

4   _____ .

10 Write.

1 Who are more intelligent, astronauts or doctors?

 <u>I think that astronauts are more intelligent than doctors.</u>

2 Which are less exciting, amusement parks or video games?

_____.

3 Is P.E. easier than music?

_____.

4 Which is more complicated, Science or Maths?

_____.

5 Which is least difficult, riding a bike or riding a horse?

_____.

6 Which is more interesting, reading a book or watching a film?

_____.

7 Which is more expensive, a car or a house?

_____.

11 Think about space. Then complete the sentences.

> amazing   complicated   interesting   expensive

1 Looking at the stars can be _____.

2 Learning about the planets is very _____.

3 Buying an astronaut outfit may be quite _____.

4 Travelling to other planets is very _____.

12 Answer the questions.

1 What things do you consider important? _____.

2 What things do you find frightening? _____.

3 What things do you think are complicated? _____.

13 Look and tick (✔).

1 Who went back in the time machine?

 **a**    **b**    **c**

2 Who went through the gates into the zoo?

 **a**    **b**    **c**

14 Read and circle.

1 Where does Serena go?

   a to the nature museum   **b** to the underground river   **c** home

2 What are the guards doing?

   a watching the show   **b** watching Serena   **c** sleeping

3 What does Serena find?

   a Champ   **b** a cage   **c** the time machine

4 Who is in a cage?

   a Zero Zendell   **b** Champ   **c** the guards

15 Write ✓ or ✗.

1 Zero Zendell was in the ads. ☐

2 Zero Zendell went into the dark jungle by himself. ☐

3 Zero Zendell said that he saved the last chimpanzee in the world. ☐

4 Marta, Chris and Serena were very unhappy. ☐

16 Read the sentences and complete the conversations.

1 I forgot my homework!

   a Oh dear! Remember it tomorrow!

   b No, you can't.

   c You should!

2 My teacher knows a lot about astronomy.

   a What is it?

   b Really? I'd like to learn more too.

   c Yes, I did.

3 What do we need to do?

   a He does our homework everyday.

   b Perhaps later.

   c We need to make a model for Science.

7

17 (3:12) **Listen and colour the sound.**

1	sm-	swam	smile	space	smell
2	sk-	street	skate	ski	Spain
3	sc-	surfing	sweet	screen	scarf
4	st-	stop	spider	storm	shop
5	sp-	spoon	speed	sky	story

18 (3:13) **Listen and write.**

S-		Es-	

19 **Read and sort the words.**

skeleton   sky   smoke   skin   smile   speak   spot   scar   strange
steak   smart   small   sports   scary   street   ski   school   screen
Spain   escape   space   eskimo   skate   skirt   statue   stripe   scorpion

sk-	sm-	st-	sp-	sc-	es-

Lesson 6 phonics and spelling (*sm-*, *st-*, *sk-*, *sp-*, *sc-*, and *s-/es-*)

20 **Read and complete.**

| curved mirror   image   concave   distorts   convex   reflects |

A mirror is a piece a glass that ¹_____ your image. There are different types of mirror and each one makes you look different. A 'normal' mirror is called a plane mirror. A ²_____ mirror is a ³_____ which ⁴_____ your ⁵_____ and makes you look short and wide. A ⁶_____ mirror makes you look very tall and thin. You can find these two types of mirror in amusement parks because they make you look funny!

21 **Read and experiment. Then write. Use words from the box.**

| long   heavy   distorted images   wide   short   thin |

Experiment with a spoon!

Take a spoon and look at the reflection of your face on both sides. Are both images the same? Explain.

1 Curved mirrors reflect _____.

2 In a convex mirror _____

_____.

3 In a concave mirror _____

_____.

22 **Read and report.**

1 **Sam:** 'In this mirror! I always look very short and heavy.'

Sam says that he _____.

2 **Betty:** 'I love this mirror because I look taller and thinner and my legs look long.'

Betty says that _____.

3 **David and Sarah:** 'We like our mirror because it reflects our real images.'

David and Sarah _____.

4 **Teacher:** 'In a convex mirror your face looks wide and short.'

The teacher _____.

Lesson 7 physical science (distorting mirrors; indirect speech, adjectives)

23 Read the texts on Pupil's Book page 79 again and complete the table.

Name and surname	Country	Main idea
	Poland	He was the first astronomer to …

24 Can you remember the planets? Look at this sentence to help you.

Most **V**ery **E**ducated **M**onkeys **J**ust **S**leep **U**nder **N**ewspapers

Mercury Venus Earth Mars Jupiter Saturn Uranus Neptune

MINI-
PROJECT

Write about an imaginary planet. What is its name? What can you see there? What does it look like?

25 Look and write.

1

_____ is he?

He's an _____.

2

_____ did he go?

He went to the _____.

3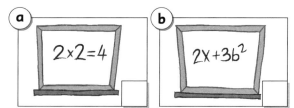

_____ did he get there?

He went by _____.

4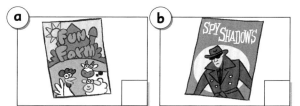

_____ is it?

It's a _____.

26 Look and tick (✓).

1 Which is more complicated?

a $2 \times 2 = 4$ b $2x + 3b^2$

2 Which is less frightening?

a FUN FOR!!   b SPY SHADOWS

3 Which is the least intelligent?

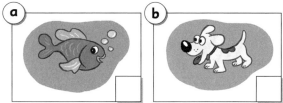

a   b

4 Which is the most important?

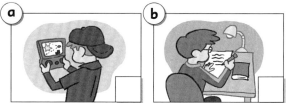

a   b

27 Read and match.

1 Where do I need to go?

2 What bus should we get to go to the city centre?

3 What can we do after the show?

4 What should I visit in London?

a You ought to see Buckingham Palace.

b You need to go the library to return the books.

c You should go home early. You have an exam tomorrow.

d You can get bus number 3. It will stop in front of the city hall.

28 Read and answer. Use your notebook.

1 Do you like astronomy? Why?

2 Have you ever used a telescope?

3 Would you like to become an astronaut? If not, what would you rather be?

4 Would you like to travel into space?

29 Match.

1 amazing

2 complicated

3 frightening

4 a telescope

5 the moon

6 satellite

a scary

b the earth has one

c difficult to understand

d not natural but goes around the earth

e use this to look at space

f really, really good

30 Write.

| more   most   less   least   first   that   important   great   second   third |

Which trainers are the best for me?

I want to buy some new trainers. There are three pairs ¹_____ I like.
The ²_____ pair are green with orange stripes. They're ³_____
but they are the ⁴_____ expensive at £105. The ⁵_____ pair are
⁶_____ expensive. They look OK but the first pair are ⁷_____
beautiful. This pair costs £75. The ⁸_____ pair are the ⁹_____
expensive at £20 but they are not a good fit. My mum says price is the most
¹⁰_____ thing. I think style is the most important thing!

31 Read and circle.

1 It's hot outside. You should (*take off / put on*) your coat.

2 You can only bring one bag. You'd (*better / better not*) bring too many things.

3 I'm worried about the exam. I (*ought to / ought not to*) talk to my teacher after school.

4 It's raining. I'd (*better / not better*) bring an umbrella.

5 I can't sleep. What (*should / had better*) I do?

I CAN I can give advice and make suggestions.
I can use adjectives to describe and compare things. ☐ ☐

8 The environment

1 Match. Then write.

paper   recycle   turn off   reuse   use   rubbish

recycle _____

collect _____

_____ bottles

_____ plastic bags

_____ public transport

_____ the lights

2 Look at the chart and complete.

1 _____ people always reuse plastic bags.

2 _____ people sometimes reuse plastic bags.

3 _____ people usually reuse plastic bags.

4 _____ people never reuse plastic bags.

5 The total number of people was _____.

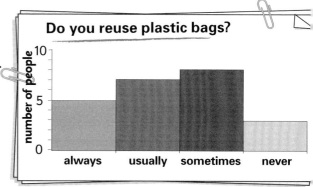

Do you reuse plastic bags?

3 Unscramble. Then write the question with *How often ...?*

1 often / she / reuses / plastic bags _____

_____ ?

2 the / never / they / use / transport / public / at / weekend

_____ .

_____ ?

3 rubbish / they / sometimes / collect / park / in / the

_____ .

_____ ?

4 🔊 3:17 **Look at Tom's plans for next week. Listen and complete.**

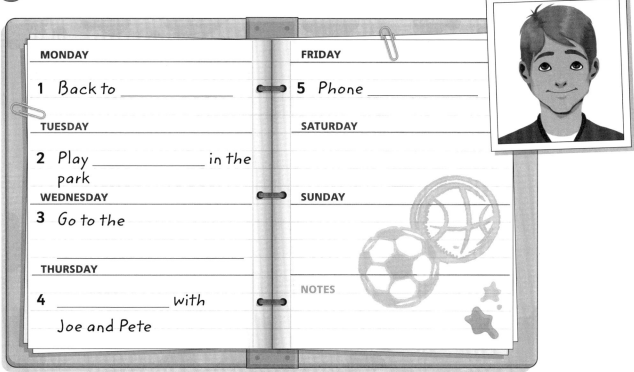

MONDAY	FRIDAY
1 Back to _____	**5** Phone _____
TUESDAY	SATURDAY
2 Play _____ in the park	
WEDNESDAY	SUNDAY
3 Go to the _____	
THURSDAY	NOTES
4 _____ with Joe and Pete	

5 **Write about yourself.**

1 What are you going to do after school?

2 What are you going to do at the weekend?

3 What are you going to do next summer?

4 What are you going to do in two hours time?

After school, I'm going to _____
_____
_____
_____
_____
_____
_____

6 **Read the questions and match.**

1 What can you do to save trees?
2 What can you do to conserve energy?
3 What can you do to save resources?
4 What can you do to keep the planet clean?

a collect rubbish.
b recycle bottles.
c recycle paper.
d turn off the lights.

7 **Write the words in the correct circle.**

waste   plastic bags   bottles   paper   pollution

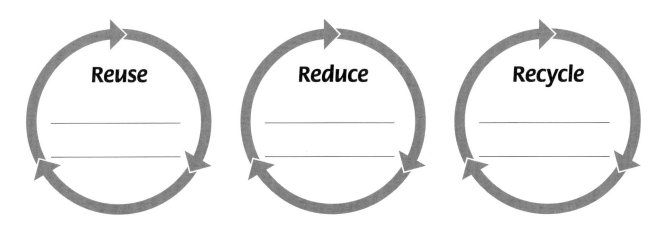

Reuse
_____
_____

Reduce
_____
_____

Recycle
_____
_____

8 **Which of the things above do you do? What about your partner?**

1 I always _____.

2 My partner always _____.

3 We both _____.

4 Neither of us _____.

9 **Look at the pictures and write sentences.**

1 I'm going to ... _____.

2 _____.

3 _____.

10 (3:21) **Listen and number.**

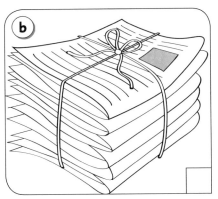

11 **Look at Activity 10 and write.**

a If you __recycle bottles__, you'll __save resources__.

b If you _____, you'll _____.

c If you _____, you'll _____.

d If you _____, you'll _____.

e If you _____, you'll _____.

f If you _____, you'll _____.

12 **Complete the sentences.**

1 If you use solar energy, _____.

2 You will reduce pollution if _____.

3 If you go camping, you should not forget to _____.

4 It will be very helpful if I _____.

5 If I reuse paper at school, _____.

Lesson 4 grammar (first conditional)

13 Look and tick (✔).

1 Who got into the cage?

 a

 b

 c

2 What can Marta and Chris use to return with Champ?

 a

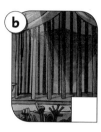 b

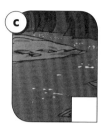 c

14 3:23 **Listen and match. Who said it?**

1 'Where were you?'

2 'We went into a time machine with Champ.'

3 'There are no real pets in the future.'

4 'He was in a cage.'

5 'We need to look after our animals.'

 a b

 c

15 Read and sort the adjectives for each character.

> brave   kind   mean   scary   interesting   dangerous   friendly
> unfriendly   unhappy   poor   lovely   horrible   fun

Champ	Marta	Serena	Zero Zendell

16 Look at the table in Activity 15. Write two sentences.

1 I think that Serena is brave because she wasn't scared of the guards.

2 _____ .

3 _____ .

(17) **Listen and write.**

> communication invasion investigation decision
> creation reduction pollution explosion
> motivation information production fiction
> action conclusion

-sion	-tion

(18) **Read and circle –*sion* in red and –*tion* in blue.**

1 Communication and information are very important in the 21st century.

2 The country is in an economic recession.

3 The reduction of pollution is necessary in our cities.

4 Students need motivation and action in their lessons.

5 It is difficult to make a decision in this situation.

6 Yesterday I watched a science fiction film.

7 There was a terrible explosion.

8 This investigation is very interesting.

(19) **Write four sentences. Use *-ion* words from Activity 17. Then read.**

1 _____.

2 _____.

3 _____.

4 _____.

20 Read and complete.

ambulance   sneeze   allergy   pollution

During your life you may suffer from an ¹_____. This is when, because of ²_____ for example, or plants and flowers, your eyes are red and you ³_____. There are different kinds of allergies and some allergies can be dangerous. If you have a very bad allergic reaction you should always call an ⁴_____ or go to the hospital. The doctor can give you medicine to help you feel better.

21 Read and match.

1 Allergies are affecting people in developed countries …

2 If you suffer from an allergy, …

3 You may have more allergies …

4 Avoid the countryside in spring …

5 If you have a severe allergic reaction, …

a … call an ambulance.

b … due to the polluted environment.

c … if you are allergic to pollen.

d … you may sneeze a lot.

e … if you live in a city or near a main road.

22 Look at the questionnaire below and answer the questions. Then complete the key.

How healthy are you?

1 Do you eat fruit every day?   Yes ☐ No ☐

2 Do you play sports?   Yes ☐ No ☐

3 Do you go to bed early?   Yes ☐ No ☐

4 Do you live in a healthy environment?   Yes ☐ No ☐

• If you have 4 'yes' answers, you _____ (be) very healthy!

• If you have 4 'no' answers, you should _____ (be) careful!

• If you have 2 or 3 'yes' or 'no' answers, you can _____ (do) better!

23 Complete the sentences.

1 If you don't take your allergy medicine _____.

2 If you don't brush your teeth _____.

3 If we don't respect the environment _____.

4 If she doesn't eat healthily _____.

24 Read the texts on Pupil's Book page 89 again. Complete the table.

Cause	→	Effect
①	→	They make us ill.
②	→	
③ Billions of tons of rubbish are produced by humans every year.	→	

25 Read and answer.

1 What can we do to stop accumulating waste?

_____.

2 What could be some ways to not pollute the air?

_____.

3 How do you do your best to protect the environment?

_____

_____

_____

_____

MINI-
PROJECT

Make a poster for your school.
Convince people to be responsible!
What should they do to take care of our environment?

26 Read and write.

> because   going to   will   must
> are   practising   dinner   I'm   next   If

Tomorrow I'm going to be home late from school ¹_____ I have band practice. This week we are ²_____ at lunchtime and after school. We are ³_____ play in a concert ⁴_____ week in the city centre. ⁵_____ going to play the clarinet and my two best friends are going to play the saxophone. ⁶_____ we play well our teacher and parents ⁷_____ be very happy. My grandparents are coming and after the concert we ⁸_____ going to go out for ⁹_____. It should be a good evening. I ¹⁰_____ practise now!

27 Remind yourself what to do where. Complete the table.

	At school	At home
RECYCLE		
REDUCE		
REUSE		

28 Complete the sentences.

1 If you use public transport, _____.

2 Separating the rubbish is important because _____.

3 You'll save water if you _____.

4 We won't have a clean planet if we _____.

5 To take care of the environment I can also _____

_____.

29 **Read and answer.**

1 Do you recycle at home? _____.

2 Do you sort the rubbish? _____.

3 How often do you use public transport? _____.

30 **Match.**

1	reduce	**a**	a poison in the environment
2	recycle	**b**	make less
3	turn off	**c**	things that are used carelessly
4	pollution	**d**	change into material that we can reuse
5	rubbish	**e**	things we throw away
6	waste	**f**	opposite of turn on

31 **Read and circle.**

I'm going to help make my school greener. My friends (*will / are going*) to help me, too.

We're going to put recycling boxes in every classroom. Then we can (*collect / turn off*)

paper and (*transport / bottles*) to recycle. My family is also going to help (*reduce / save*)

energy at home. They're going to (*use / turn off*) the lights when they go out,

and my mum is going to (*use / reuse*) public transport to go to the supermarket.

32 **Unscramble and write. Then match.**

1 public / transport / if / you / use

_____

2 you / recycle / if / paper

_____

3 the / off / lights / if / you / turn

_____

4 recycle / if / bottles / you

_____

a you'll save resources.

b you'll conserve energy.

c you'll reduce pollution.

d you'll save trees.

 I CAN

I can talk about ways to help the environment. ☐

I can talk about what I'm going to do in the future. ☐

I can use and understand sentences with conditionals. ☐

1 Read and circle *True* (T) or *False* (F).

1 Marta is back from the future and lives with her parents. T / F

2 Champ is now living in the future with Zero Zendell. T / F

3 Chris is back in school studying hard. T / F

4 Serena is on Future Island walking her dog every day. T / F

5 Zero Zendell doesn't have a zoo now. T / F

6 There aren't any visitors to the zoo now. T / F

2 Look at the pictures and answer.

1 Whose is this?

_____

2 Why did he take it to the camp?

_____

3 What is in the photo?

_____

4 Whose it is?

_____

5 Who is on the bus?

_____

6 What can they see from the bus? _____

3 Read and match.

1 Were there any animals on Future Island?

2 What was Zero Zendell like?

3 Did the guards lock up Champ?

4 Who used the river to enter the zoo?

5 How did Serena break the cage?

6 Who got Champ from the stage?

a Yes, they did.

b Yes, there were but they were all in Zero Zendell's zoo.

c She used the time machine.

d He was a horrible man.

e Marta.

f Serena.

4 Write. What is traditional in your country?

In my country we have got many traditions. We eat ¹_____.
We also like music. We listen to ²_____. If you come
here, you should see ³_____. Don't forget to visit
⁴_____. You'll enjoy it!

5 Find these time words.

m	i	d	n	i	g	h	t	a	b	d	t	a	h
c	r	e	f	d	j	y	k	t	p	l	d	l	k
l	q	t	o	m	o	r	r	o	w	q	e	a	z
u	m	i	n	p	s	r	y	n	p	y	i	t	s
z	c	m	i	n	u	t	e	i	r	d	e	e	p
m	r	e	f	z	l	u	x	g	a	a	s	r	o
i	q	a	r	j	p	r	e	h	p	t	y	a	z
d	k	a	q	z	n	e	x	t	w	e	e	k	e
d	u	y	p	r	n	l	b	y	j	f	a	z	x
a	h	a	l	f	a	n	h	o	u	r	r	m	p
y	o	l	c	t	d	a	d	k	v	p	b	x	c
n	u	a	m	a	n	d	p	m	n	o	s	r	h
v	r	l	s	q	v	c	y	m	n	b	q	p	p

tomorrow
later
tonight
half an hour
next week
time
am and pm
midday
midnight
hour
minute
date
year

6 Ask and write. Complete for yourself and your partner.

	Me	My partner
Name and surname		
Favourite food		
Favourite sport		
Favourite animal		
Hobbies		

7 Look and write.

My past

1 Last summer, I _____ .

2 Yesterday, I _____ by myself.

3 I've never _____ .

My present

4 I'm good at _____ .

5 I like _____ , but I don't like _____ .

6 I love _____ and _____ .

7 I can _____ , but I can't _____ .

8 There is a _____ near my house.

9 I want to _____ .

10 I have to _____ .

My future

11 Tomorrow when I get up, first I _____ .

12 Then, I _____ .

13 Next year, I _____ .

14 If I work hard at school, I _____ .

8 Draw a picture of your town or city. Label each place.

shopping centre
museum   post office
chemist   circus
theatre   cinema
college   factory
newsagent
school   bookshop
bus stop   stadium
police station
underground   park

9 Read and complete the sentences.

when   where   why   how   which   what   who

1 _____ are you happy?

2 _____ is that bright light?

3 _____ is the most frightening?

4 _____ is your favourite film star?

5 _____ do you live?

6 _____ do you get up?

7 _____ did you get here?

10 Draw a poster about how to help the environment. Then write.

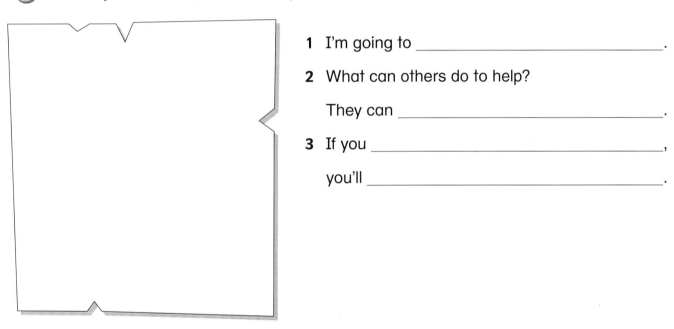

1 I'm going to _____.

2 What can others do to help?

They can _____.

3 If you _____,

you'll _____.

11 Write a goodbye poem.

G _____

O _____

O _____

D _____

B _____

Y _____

E _____

Bonfire Night

1 **Look and match.**

 **a**    **b**    **c**     **d**

1 James I was the King of England. ☐

2 Guy Fawkes. He didn't like the King. ☐

3 The Houses of Parliament, London. ☐

4 The guards. ☐

2 (3:33) **Listen. Then number the sentences.**

How Guy Fawkes' plan failed

☐ On the 5th of November, guards found Guy Fawkes in the basement. The King and the Houses of Parliament were safe!

☐ Guy and his friends knew about explosives. They wanted to put gunpowder in barrels in the basement of the Houses of Parliament on November the 5th, 1605.

☐ In 1603, James I became the new King of England. Not everybody in England liked him.

☐ The King received an anonymous letter about the plot.

☐ A man called Guy Fawkes and his friends wanted to blow up the Houses of Parliament with the King inside.

3 **Read and match.**

1 When do they celebrate Bonfire Night in the UK?

2 Why is Bonfire Night important in the British calendar?

3 What do people do on Bonfire Night?

a People have bonfires and they watch fireworks. It's fun!

b Bonfire Night takes places every year on November 5th.

c Bonfire Night celebrates how Guy Fawkes' plan failed.

4 **Answer these questions.**

1 Do people have bonfires and fireworks in your country? _____

2 When do people have bonfires and fireworks? _____

3 What are people celebrating? _____

Christmas Crackers

5 Read the text on Pupil's Book page 98 again and answer the questions.

1 Who invented the Christmas cracker? _____.

2 What is a Christmas cracker? _____.

3 How does a Christmas cracker snap? _____.

4 What can you find inside a Christmas cracker? _____.

6 Read and number the sentences.

a Get some Christmas wrapping paper. ☐

b Put the note, joke and small gift inside. ☐

c Tie both ends. ☐

d Your Christmas cracker is ready to pull! ☐

e Make a small gift for your friend. ☐

f Write a joke. ☐

g Save a toilet paper roll from home. 1

h Cover the roll with the wrapping paper. ☐

7 Write a joke for your Christmas cracker.

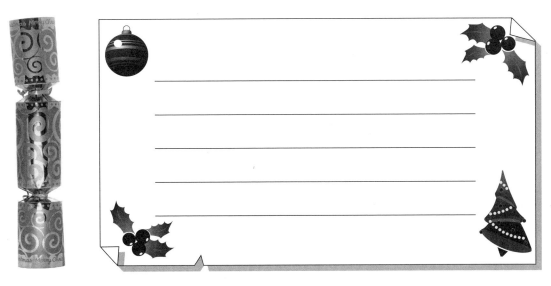

Easter Eggs

8 (3:38) **Listen and number.**

a Egg decorating ☐

b Egg Rolling ☐

c Egg Hunt ☐

d Egg presents ☐

9 **Read the instructions. Write _Yes_ or _No_.**

How to make Sticker Easter Eggs

1 Fill a swimming pool ½ to ¾ full of milk. _____

2 Add a tablespoon of vinegar. _____

3 Add some pencils until you like the colour! _____

4 Put the stickers on the eggs. _____

5 Let it boil for 15 days. _____

6 Remove from heat. _____

7 Remove the eggs and keep them wet. _____

8 Leave the stickers on the eggs. _____

10 **Think of a dish made with hard-boiled eggs. Draw your dish. Write the recipe.**

Wimbledon

11 **Read and complete.**

> 1877   London   summer   July   player   then

Every summer, a traditional tennis event takes place in ¹_____ in the last week of June and the first week of ²_____. Perhaps you have seen a tennis ³_____ from your country playing on the Wimbledon grass. The first championship took place in ⁴_____. Since ⁵_____, Wimbledon has been part of British ⁶_____ entertainment.

12 **Read. Then circle *True* or *False*.**

1 A lot of people wait in a queue to spend a day at Wimbledon.   True / False

2 Married ladies are called 'Miss'.   True / False

3 Tennis players always wear white.   True / False

4 People have strawberries with cream.   True / False

5 Wimbledon is not on TV.   True / False

13 **(3:41) Listen and complete.**

> taxi   underground   bus   train

1 If you get the _____, the nearest stop to the grounds is Southfields station.

2 If you go to Waterloo Station, you can get a _____ to Wimbledon station.

3 If you take _____ number 493 from Richmond, it will go directly to the grounds.

4 You can always get a _____ to Wimbledon if you are in London.

Review

Welcome & Unit 1

1 **Read and sort. How often do you see these professionals?**

> pilot policeman/woman waiter singer actor secretary singer
> gardener hairdresser nurse receptionist tour guide chemist dentist

Never	Sometimes	Usually

2 **Write the question tag.**

1 Your mum is a secretary, _____?

2 They work at a restaurant, but they aren't waiters, _____?

3 The lady at the reception is the receptionist, _____?

4 The pilot isn't late for our flight, _____?

3 **Read and circle.**

1 You wash your hands (*before* / *after*) you eat.
2 You brush your teeth (*before* / *after*) you eat.
3 I can read a compass (*but* / *so*) I can't light a fire.
4 It's not raining (*but* / *so*) we can play outside.

4 **Read and complete.**

> friendly rough round sweet soft

1 An orange feels _____. It looks _____ and it tastes _____.

2 My cat looks _____. He feels _____.

Unit 2

1 Read and write.

1 People can see butterflies in the rainforest.

<u>Butterflies can be seen in the rainforest.</u>

2 Scientists rescue animals in wild parks.

_____ are rescued by _____ in wild parks.

3 People can't find turtles in this city.

_____ can't be _____ in this city.

4 Visitors can see whales in the ocean.

_____.

2 Read and unscramble.

1 bigger / seals / otters / are / than   _____?

2 heaviest / the / hippo / is / the   _____?

3 trees / houses / were / taller / the / than   _____?

3 Read and complete.

1 Giraffes are _____ (tall) than turtles.

2 Hippos are _____ (heavy) than tigers.

3 Turtles are the _____ (slow) animals in the ocean.

4. Tigers are _____ (brave) than monkeys.

4 Read. Then match.

1 Birds use this part of their body to fly.   a butterfly

3 A big type of bird with a long neck that lives on rivers or lakes.   b extinct

5 The hair that covers the body of an animal.   c fur

2 An insect with wings and beautiful colours.   d octopus

4 A sea animal with eight long arms called tentacles.   e swan

6 Doesn't exist now.   f wing

Unit 3

1 Read and complete.

1 If you _____ (go) to France, you will _____ (see) the Eiffel Tower.

2 You _____ (get) to the city centre faster, if you _____ (walk).

3 She _____ (buy) new clothes, if she _____ (find) the shopping centre.

4 If the circus _____ (come) to town, _____ (enjoy) the clowns.

2 Read. Then circle.

1 You (*should* / *shouldn't*) visit the museum. It's very interesting.

2 You (*have to* / *should*) take some cash with you. The bus does not take credit cards.

3 If you want to go to the cinema, you (*need to* / *will*) get the underground. It's too far away!

4 I (*want to* / *need to*) go to the stadium. I have to buy a T-shirt for my mum.

3 Read and answer. Then write about you.

1 Where did you use to live when you were little?

I used to _____.

2 What games did you use to play?

I used to _____.

3 What places did you use to go to?

I used to _____.

4 Read. Then choose the correct word.

| circus   bridge   university   theatre   stadium   underground   factory   corner |

1 A place where people can see a play.

2 A place where you can see clowns, acrobats and animals.

3 A system of trains running under the surface.

4 A large building with no roof where you can see a sport.

5 A place where people study for a degree.

6 A building where people make things with machines.

7 You can cross a river if you go over this.

8 The place where two walls meet.

Unit 4

1 Write the questions.

1 _____? I cooked some stew.

2 _____? They had lunch in a restaurant.

3 _____? No, he didn't.

4 _____? She put the salad in the fridge.

2 Read and circle.

1 My mum made my favourite food, spaghetti. She made me so (*happy* / *soft* / *foggy*).

2 It makes me (*sad* / *hungry* / *proud*) when we talk about food!

3 The mud made the kitchen (*dirty* / *clean* / *cold*).

4 Walking a lot can make you (*thirsty* / *cloudy* / *embarrassed*).

3 Complete these sentences.

1 Yesterday my dad cooked fish and chips while I _____ (watch) TV.

2 I _____ (wait) for two hours, but he never came.

3 What _____ (she / do) at 5 o'clock last night?

4 You _____ (not / study) when we called.

4 Read. Then match.

knife   fork   meal   spoon   husband   chopsticks   wife   surname   pepper

1 A grey powder to make food hot and spicy   a   pepper

2 This is what you use to eat soup   b _____

3 This is what you use to cut or spread food   c _____

4 The food or the time when you eat food   d _____

5 A man who is married   e _____

6 A woman who is married   f _____

7 A small object with four points to pick up food with   g _____

8 A pair of narrow sticks to eat Asian food   h _____

9 Your last name   i _____

Unit 5

1 **Read. Then write the question tag.**

1 You enjoyed the concert, _____?

2 They didn't watch the show, _____?

3 Felipe didn't go to the cinema by himself, _____?

4 You bought a new piano, _____?

2 **Read. Then complete.**

> since   for   yet   already

1 I've lived here _____ 3 years.

2 She's learned many things _____ she started to read.

3 We haven't been to that restaurant _____.

4 Have you _____ practised for the concert?

3 **Read. Then complete.**

1 I _____ (talk) to James, when the telephone _____ (ring).

2 We _____ (walk) to the shopping centre, when we _____ (see) our bus.

3 They _____ (have) lunch, when somebody _____ (knock) at the door.

4 She _____ (play) with her sister, when it _____ (start) to rain.

4 **Read. Then write the correct word.**

> metal   paper   plastic   glass

1 Some flowers that are not real can be made of this. _____

2 Windows and bottles are made of this. _____

3 Newspapers and books are made of this. _____

4 A type of material that is very hard and often shiny. _____

Unit 6

1 **Answer these questions about your next holiday. Then write.**

1 Where will you go?   **2** Who will you go with?   **3** How long will you stay?
4 What will you see?   **5** What will you do?

For my next holiday _____
_____
_____
_____
_____

2 **Write the questions using *shall* or *what else*.**

1 <u>Shall we go to the cinema</u> ? Yes, I'd love to go to the cinema.

2 _____ ? We could also go to castle after we eat lunch.

3 _____ ? Maybe not. I've seen pyramids before.

4 _____ ? What about making a snowman after we ski?

3 **Read and circle.**

1 You (*may* / *has* / *do*) be right.
2 Visitors (*have* / *may* / *make*) only enter one at a time.
3 She (*will* / *might* / *can*) go to the party. She's not too sure.
4 I (*have* / *might* / *do*) pass the test. I knew most of the answers.

4 **Read and match.**

> journey   envelope   stamp   diary   guidebook   ~~suitcase~~   storm

1 This is where you carry your clothes when you travel. <u>suitcase</u>
2 A book with information about a city, country or continent. _____
3 The act of travelling from one place to another. _____
4 A small piece of paper with a picture that you put on letters. _____
5 A book where you write about your feelings. _____
6 This is the place where you put a letter. _____
7 A type of weather with lots of wind, rain, thunder and lightning. _____

Unit 7

1 Read and circle.

1 You (*shouldn't* / *need to*) watch TV so much.

2 They (*could* / *'d better*) stay at home if they want.

3 She (*ought to* / *will*) learn about stars. It's fun!

4 (*Shouldn't* / *Ought to*) we turn off the lights to see the stars?

5 We'd (*better* / *could*) go or we will miss the bus.

2 Read and think. Do you agree? Write ✓ or ✗ .

1 Science is less complicated than Maths. ☐

2 Earth is more interesting than Pluto. ☐

3 Being an astronaut is more dangerous than being a teacher. ☐

4 Flying is more expensive than taking a train. ☐

5 Learning is the most important thing at school. ☐

3 Read and complete the table.

"It is cloudy today."	He says it is cloudy today.
"The teacher is very friendly."	She says
"We are getting hungry."	They say
"It will be expensive."	You say
"We are going to the zoo."	We say

4 Read and match.

1	Something that weighs a lot.	a	long
2	Something that is not fantasy.	b	short
3	Something that is certain.	c	sure
4	Something that is small in length.	d	heavy
5	Something that is the opposite of short.	e	real

Unit 8

1 Answer the questions. Then write.

1 Where are you going to go at the weekend?

2 Who are you going to meet?

3 What fun things are you going to do?

4 What food are you going to eat?

This weekend ...
_____
_____
_____
_____
_____
_____
_____

2 Read and circle.

1 the / rains / if / cancelled / match / be / will / it

2 clean / dirty / they / house / will / if / the / is / it

3 call / will / I / if / school / the / late / am / I

4 very / team / we / be / wins / excited / if / will / our

3 Read and match.

1 If I remember his number

2 If the weather is good

3 If we go to the rainforest

4 If we all use public transport

5 If I'm not too tired

a there will be less pollution.

b I will call him.

c we will play outside.

d I will go to the sports club.

e we will see lots of animals.

4 Read and match.

1 Good for you.

2 A special vehicle to take people to hospital.

3 Not feeling well.

4 Not dirty.

5 Something you take to feel better.

a medicine

b ambulance

c ill

d healthy

e clean

Picture Dictionary

Unit 1 Adventure camp

Camping equipment

sleeping bag

tent

rucksack

pegs

compass

torch

campsite

fire

Camping activities

pitch the tent

take down
the tent

put in the
pegs

lay out the
bed

cover our
heads

light a fire

keep out the
rain

read a
compass

Deforestation

river

sea

before

after

deforestation

Unit 2 Wildlife park

Wild animals

rhino   cheetah   panther   lemur   camel

whale   seal   otter   turtle   tiger

Superlative adjectives

tallest   longest   shortest   biggest   smallest

heaviest   lightest   fastest   slowest

Fossils

dinosaur   fossil   swan   octopus

Unit 3 Where we live

City places

shopping centre

post office

cinema

chemist

newsagent

college

circus

factory

theatre

university

airport

bookshop

fire station

police station

railway station

bus stop

guest house

stadium

underground

Directions

left

right

urban

rural

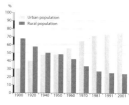
population

north

south

east

west

Unit 4 · Good and bad days

International food

curry

omelette

spaghetti

fish and chips

paella

dumplings

sushi

stew

rice and beans

Verbs and objects

pack my bag

miss the bus

pass a test

open a lunchbox

remember my juice

drop the ball

Health

nutrients

sedentary

physical activity

vitamins

minerals

Unit 5 Arts and entertainment

Types of films

thriller

comedy

sci-fi

romance

musical

cartoon

Instruments

cello

harmonica

saxophone

triangle

drums

clarinet

harp

tambourine

Types of music

rock

blues

country

pop

jazz

Unit 6 Trips

Tourist attractions

museum

aquarium

amusement
park/theme park

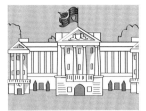
palace

water park

castle

National
Park

Amusement park attractions

go on the big
wheel

go on the
dodgems

play mini-golf

go on the
carousel

go on the
boating lake

go on the
pirate ship

go on the
water slide

go on the
rollercoaster

The weather

snow

rain

drought

fog

storm

Unit 7 Space

Space

astronaut

planet

telescope

alien

spaceship

comet

satellite

rocket

boosters

space station

Adjectives

complicated

amazing

frightening

intelligent

brilliant

important

interesting

expensive

horrible

Distorting mirrors

concave

convex

reflect

distorted image

curved mirror

Unit 8 The environment

Ways to help the environment

recycle paper

recycle bottles

collect rubbish

reuse plastic bags

reduce waste

turn off the lights

Environmentally friendly outcomes

save trees

save resources

keep the
planet clean

conserve energy

reduce pollution

use public transport

Allergies

allergies

pollution

sneezing

ambulance

Pearson Education Limited
Edinburgh Gate
Harlow
Essex CM20 2JE
England
and Associated Companies throughout the world.

www.islands.pearson.com

First published 2012
Eighth impression 2018
ISBN: 978-1-4082-9079-8

Set in Fiendstar 12.5/15pt
Printed in Slovakia by Neografia

Based on the work of Megan Roderick, John Wiltshier and José Luis Morales

Picture Credits

The Publisher would like to thank the following for their kind permission to reproduce their photographs:

(Key: b-bottom; c-centre; l-left; r-right; t-top)

Alamy Images: adrian davies 24 (1), Alex Segre 106 (bookshop), 107 (fish & chips), British Retail Photography 28 (3), 106 (chemist), Colin Underhill 30 (3), 106 (airport), Craig Lovell / Eagle Visions Photography 108 (jazz), Design Pics Inc. – RM Content 25 (b), / F1online digitale Bildagentur GmbH 109 (fog), GeoPhotos 28 (1), 106 (factory), Haje Jan Kamps 28 (4), 106 (college), Ian Canham 30 (4), 106 (university), Image Source 111 (allergy), imagebroker 25 (c), Jon Sparks 15bc, Justin Kase zsixz 106 (police station), Lin-Ann Lim 30 (1), 106 (underground), Mark Mercer 106 (bus stop), Myrleen Pearson 25 (a), ncamerastock 106 (post office), Olli Geibel 109 (storm), Paul King 107 (curry), Photocuisine 107 (omelette), Photoshot Holdings Ltd 104 (deforestation), Russell Kord 106 (guest house), SHOUT 110 (curved mirror), Simon Attrill 15br, Terry Whittaker 104 (after), Tetra Images 109 (snow), The Photolibrary Wales 106 (fire station), 106 (stadium), Thomas Cockrem 15 (b); **Corbis:** Blend Images / Ariel Skelley 109 (boating lake), Eye Ubiquitous / David Batterbury 109 (pirate ship), Monalyn Gracia 110 (reflect), Science Faction / Steven Kazlowski 25b;

Fotolia.com: aldaer 26, Alexander Kazhdan 111 (pollution), Andrey Armyagov 107 (vitamins), Anton Prado PHOTO 109 (drought), arbaes 28 (7), 106 (theatre), david hughes 104 (river), Eric Isselée 105 (camel), Friday 104 (sea), hazel proudlove 107 (minerals), liping dong 24 (3), 105 (dinosaur), Monkey Business 107 (sedentary), Olga Lyubkin 107 (nutrients), Peter Baxter 106 (circus), Silkstock 93, Skogas 107 (physical activity), styleuneed 108 (drums), TA Craft Photography 111 (ambulance), xstockerx 105 (swan), Yevgenia Gorbulsky 109 (rain); **Getty Images:** John Arnold / John Cancalosi 105 (fossil), Stone / Anthony Boccaccio 104 (before), UpperCut Images / Zave Smith 15 (c), WireImage / Venturelli 9 (a); **iStockphoto:** Eric Isselée 105 (cheetah), Ismael Montero Verdu 24 (2), John Rodriguez 24 (4), kali9 16, Trent Chambers 111 (sneeze), Valerii Kaliuzhnyi 105 (rhino); **Ottmar Bierwagen:** 24 (6), 105 (octopus); **Pearson Education Ltd:** Jules Selmes 11, Tudor Photography 30b; **Press Association Images:** EMPICS Entertainment / PictureGroup / Gregg 9 (d), PA Wire / David Davies 9 (c); **Rex Features:** 28 (2), 106 (newsagent), Brian Rasic 108 (pop), Courtesy Everett Collection 108 (blues), Jim Smeal / BEI 108 (country), Newspix 108 (rock), Patrick Frilet 15bl, Sipa Press 9 (b); **Shutterstock.com:** Adisa 107 (sushi), Africa Studio 109 (big wheel), Alex James Bramwell 105 (turtle), Anat-oli 105 (shortest), Andrea Skjold 107 (dumplings), Anne Kitzman 109 (mini golf), Benis Arapovic 109 (water slide), Brett Mulcahy 107 (stew), Cardiae 105 (lightest), Cathy Keifer 24 (5), Christopher Elwell 105 (seal), Comosaydice 21 (turtle), Computer Earth 105 (biggest), 105 (whale), Devi 109 (dodgems), Dmitry Skutin 108 (harp), Dmitry Vereshchagin 108 (tambourine), Dusan964 105 (slowest), Eddtoro 76 (1), Elena Schweitzer 108 (triangle), Enshpil 108 (harmonica), Eric Isselée 105 (fastest), 105 (otter), 105 (panther), Evgeniy Ayupov 105 (smallest), F. Krause 108 (saxophone), Fivespots 105 (longest), Four Oaks 27 (3), Ivan Kuzmin 21 (rhino), Jan Kratochvila 27 (1), Jerry Zitterman 109 (rollercoaster), Jose Antonio Perez 76 (3), Karel Gallas 27 (4), Kayros Studio 76 (4), Kletr 105 (tallest), Konstantin Sutyagin 76 (2), Lalito 108 (clarinet), Marie Lumiere 27 (2), Monkey Business Images 107 (rice &beans), NREY 105 (Lemur), Pandapaw 105 (tiger), Paul Banton 21 (giraffe), Peter Zurek 28 (6), 106 (cinema), Photobar 21 (cheetah), Prism68 28 (5), 106 (shopping centre), Richard Peterson 105 (heaviest), RM 21 (whale), Robert Ford 109 (carousel), Robyn Mackenzie 108 (cello), Szefei 51, Tracy Whiteside 15 (a), Ungor 30 (2), 106 (railway station); **Thinkstock:** istockphoto 107 (paella), 107 (spaghetti)

All other images © Pearson Education

Every effort has been made to trace the copyright holders and we apologise in advance for any unintentional omissions. We would be pleased to insert the appropriate acknowledgement in any subsequent edition of this publication.

Illustration Acknowledgements
Illustrated by Charlotte Alder (The Bright Agency), Fred Blunt, Moreno Chiacchiera (Beehive Illustration), Lawrence Christmas, Leo Cultura, Mark Draisey, HL Studios, Sue King (Plum Pudding Illustration), John Martz, Simone Massoni (Advocate Art), Rob McClurkan (Beehive Illustration), Ken Mok, Olimpia Wong